Becky Lovejoy   Photo by John Garcia

About the Author:

Becky Lovejoy is an educator and writer. She is the author of collections of essays, illustrated calendars, workbooks and other creative projects that focus on the natural world and spirituality. She has a Master's Degree in Higher Education and is a Certified Interpretive Guide, and works with organizations that preserve, protect and educate about the flora and fauna of our planet. The Oregon Zoo has ignited her passion for educating the public about zoos and for fundraising to support zoo conservation and research efforts. A transplant from Arizona, she now calls the Northwest her home.

About the Cover Artist:

Julia Loyd is a teacher and artist who lives on a remote island near Vancouver, British Columbia. She works in a variety of media, including watercolor, paper cutting, fabric, photography, and music composition. Her work is informed by the natural world of her region and by folk art. A partial gallery is at queenjulia.org/gallery/gallery.html. Contact her at art@queenjulia.org.

Julie Loyd   Photo by Camilla Loyd

ZOO ESSAYS: WONDERING AND WANDERING AT THE OREGON ZOO. © 2004 by Rebecca Lovejoy. All Rights Reserved. No part of this book may be reproduced without written permission from the author, except for brief quotations for critical articles and reviews.

For information, write to Murray Blvd #107, Portla
la-beck@juno.com

Becky Lovejoy
1380 NW 137th Ave
Portland, OR 97229-4414

Printed by ADPRINT Company, Portland, Oregon.
www.adprintcompany.com
(503) 771-1181

Lovejoy, Rebecca, 1960-
    Zoo Tales: Wondering and Wandering at the Oregon Zoo

1. Animals   2. Nature   3. Animal – Human Relationships   4. Zoo Animals
ISBN: 0-9760060-0-6

First Printing 2004
1 2 3 4 5 6 7 8 9 10

Zoo Tales: Wondering & Wandering at the Oregon Zoo

Becky Lovejoy

Written by Becky Lovejoy

Cover art by Julia Loyd

Pavo Press
Portland, Oregon

Disclaimer

This book is a work of fiction. Events that are based on true experiences may have been modified to support the story line. Names of people have been changed but animal names are generally accurate as of the time of printing. The author and the Oregon Zoo are held harmless from any acts of omission or any inaccuracies within these pages and the telling of these tales.

Dedication

This book is dedicated to the staff, volunteers, visitors and financial supporters of the Oregon Zoo and zoos all over North America, and applauds their tireless efforts on behalf of the animal kingdom.

A portion of the profits supports the Oregon Zoo's *Campaign for Condors* and other efforts that help to create a better future for wildlife.

Simply put, this book was written for those already committed to the preservation of wildlife, and to those who are about to be.

Oregon Zoo, 2004

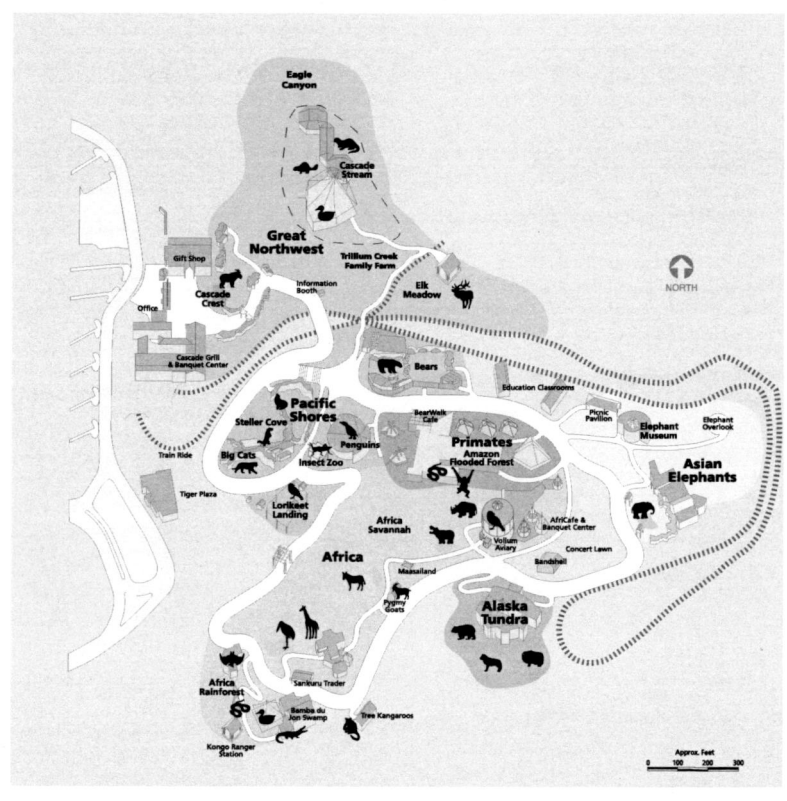

Table of Contents:

Preface vi
Acknowledgements viii
You Don't See This Every Day 1
Croc Talk 15
Connecting with the Creatures 23
Proud Tigers and Lonely Bears 33
Wapiti Wisdom 43
Care of the Long-Necks 51
Wild Spaces for Wild Things 65
E-Mails Home 79
Snowy Owls and the Good Life 91
Taxonomy or Tenderness? 103
Eagle Canyon 109
The Whitening of Water 119
A Trunk-full of Knowledge 131
Which is More Precious? 149
Above All Else, Be Kind 159
Messages From The Deep 171

Preface

Why write a book? Why write about the zoo? Why write it now? It comes down to imagination, insight and inspiration. Here's how it happened....

A little over a year ago, my mom innocently handed me John Sedgwick's book: <u>The Peaceful Kingdom: A Year in the Life of America's Oldest Zoo</u>. What fun! I figured I could write something like it and my imagination took off. A month later I was on my hands and knees in the snowy owl exhibit at the Oregon Zoo, doing work as a horticulture volunteer. It was fascinating being inside an exhibit instead of looking at it from the other side of the railing. A stray conversation with a zoo visitor and a thoughtful exchange of stares with an owl gave me insights that compelled me to write.

Imagination and insight are well and good, but it took one last encounter to push me over the edge to commit and write an entire book. I became a "keeper talk" groupie, listening to the scheduled talks in the summer and pestering the keepers with questions. Jeb Barsh, one of our elephant keepers, gave an inspiring talk that said our generation might be the last one to see elephants in the wild. It was an "ah ha" moment for me. It brought home how critical our caring and stewardship is to endangered animals in zoos and in the wild, and I now had inspiration — this is important work and there is no time to lose.

Passion for our world is important, as well as committed action on behalf of all the life with which we share the planet. This book is about my love for animals and green growing things, the verdant beauty of the Northwest, and an amazing inspiration — the Oregon Zoo.

My goal for this book is to bring you closer to the life before you. Breathe some of the same air that whooshes out of the nostrils of a Steller sea lion as he surfaces to breathe, watch a 12,000-pound elephant delicately pick sunflower seeds up with his trunk, and feel the air from the wingtips of a Harris hawk as she flies low overhead on her way to the stage at the bird show. My wish for you is to be inspired to love and protect those you meet at a zoo or in these pages. I hope you'll feel connected to the primates who look and act so much like you, but also reach out to the poison dart frogs, the buckeye butterfly, and the saddle-bill stork, and find the heart in them that beats with a similar rhythm to yours.

Acknowledgements

I used to skip over acknowledgement sections in books myself, but not any more. It's really true that it takes a herd, a tribe or an entire village to write a book, and it's fascinating to see how it all comes together. Here are the folks who were instrumental in getting this book off the ground and into your waiting hands.

First and foremost, John Garcia, my lifelong friend and inspiration. He applauded my persistence of which I have a steady supply, and helped me find patience when I was running out. He's made numerous trips to the Northwest to help me with all aspects of editing, publishing and marketing. A steady stream of bulky packages filled with books, clippings and letters of encouragement have bridged the geographic distance between us, and have kept the creative juices humming.

Imagination, insight and inspiration were the keys to committing to this book. Esther Norris, my mom, gave me the zoo book that inspired me to write this one. Linda Coady-Richardson, Mike Watson and Rick Hanes of the Oregon Zoo horticulture staff participated in the horticulture volunteer program that led me to a moment of insight in the snowy owl exhibit and started me to put words on the page. Jeb Barsh, elephant keeper, gave me the last nudge of inspiration so I could commit to and complete the book with a sense of urgency and purpose.

The zoo community was 100% behind this effort, and supported this book in many ways. ZooGuides Peggy Dale, Debbie King, Gloria Koch, Katherine Lloyd-Knox, Jennie McKee, Candace Schryver, Tom Nelson, Amy Sinclair and Mary Veronda, helped me feel at home at the zoo and inspired my writing and thinking. Krist Sandness and the staff of the ZooSnooze program gave me an insider's peek at education programs for children, and Roger Yerke and Rex Ettlin of the Education Department gave me training and information to give substance to the book. The Horticulture Department gave me great experiences on the grounds to write about, and wonderful stories about the history of the zoo. Anissa Morello and Krista Swan of the Marketing Department gave me a taste of what goes into the opening of an exhibit, as we worked on the Eagle Canyon opening. Michael Illig, Senior Keeper of North America, and Jan Mothershed, Animal Registrar and Animal Information Specialist, provided accurate historical information and insights into zoo philosophy. Mike Keele, Deputy Director, provided background on the zoo's conservation and research efforts. Terri Pelham, General Manager of the gift shop, was enthusiastic about carrying and promoting the book. Teri Dresler, Assistant Director, welcomed me into the zoo family by supporting this project and paving the way for promoting the book. Tony Vecchio, Zoo Director, received bits and pieces of this book in his mailbox and sent encouraging handwritten notes that I taped by my desk to keep me going.

The Oregon Zoo's volunteer program is one of the finest in North America, in the huge number of people who participate and in the exceptional variety of activities one can take part in. Paula McCall, Volunteer Program Manager, led me to the ZooGuide volunteer program, encouraged my writing, found talented people to review my manuscript, and then paved the way to get the book out to staff and volunteers. Sara Laursen, Volunteer Program Coordinator, provided opportunities for me to do horticulture work and opening day activities for Eagle Canyon, prepare condor nests for those amazing birds, and learn to drive zoo vehicles without major mishaps.

Ten people reviewed the manuscript and gave generously of their time to make this book better all around: Diane Cooper, Peggy Dale, Teri Dresler, John Garcia, Helen Hiczun, Nancy Kluss, Julie Loyd, Jennie McKee, Tracy Modde and Linda Waltmire. I was braced to defend my work against their red pens, but was bowled over with their constructive insights, thankful for their systematic attention to grammar and style, and grateful beyond belief for the myriad of bloopers they caught before the book went to press. I had tigers prancing around in the Serengeti, Gandhi wearing a sari, and birds flying in the northwest that have never been seen outside of Florida. Sometimes you get so creative that your brains fall out! They were here to catch me, brains and all.

Thanks to good friends who helped over this last year and a half: Barbara Blossom Ashmun reminded me to have a ledger column that measures happiness when publishing a book; Elaine DeLuca encouraged me to live this dream; Sandi Fitts-Freeman provided monkey and otter mascots to cheer me on; "Judy" provided company, steadfastness, and a dog's unconditional love while I typed into the night; Len Laviolette allowed himself to be caught up in my enthusiasm and dragged to the Zoo innumerable times; Eileen Preston dropped copies of my essays at the front door with corrections and encouragement; and Steven Augustine and Roy Rasera helped me with various aspects of business and technology. My Tucson friends were also here in spirit with suggestions and support: Diana Lett, Don and Maxine McLean, Celese Rei, Shelie Romero and Lisa Romero.

A big thanks to people in groups I've participated in. "The Tribe" is a spiritual group and Phil Marsh, Sandi Fitts-Freeman and Chris Ruddy have helped me reflect, contemplate, and re-think ways to be in the world. The "Success Team" is a goal-setting group and Paula Pierce and Kathleen Lansing have been privy to every detail of my journey and cheered me on in the pursuit of a balanced life. "The Herd" is a virtual community that I created by e-mailing 25 friends on a regular basis with my writings as I completed them. A herd is a group of creatures that have a common bond, stick together, and help the survival of the group. They have been this for me and more. A shortened list now hears about the publishing, sales and marketing end of the business, and provides input and focus to my efforts.

Family is always critical. Esther Norris, my mom, provided insight and unconditional love as well as prodigious amounts of scratch paper for the mountains of drafts these essays produced before their final form. Fred Norris, my late father, would be proud to see that the ream of blank paper he gave me for Christmas one year, has indeed ended up as a book, decades later. My sister, Jenn Bush, got me started at the zoo by telling me about the horticulture volunteer program. She also gave me a towering stack of info from the 1980's when she was a ZooGuide, providing me endless material to pique my interest and then to draw from. My other sister, Julie Loyd, gave me focused feedback and basic pointers on how to write, lots of encouragement when I needed it most, and the amazing art you see on the cover.

Portland printers from Adprint Company, Tim Trachtenberg and Tim Carp, took on this project eagerly and helped me learn the ropes. I promised them Rolaids while we're printing, and champagne once we're finished, and look forward to having stacks of books in my living room for the next few months.

Thanks in advance to all the people who will be involved in the promotion and sales process, and for those of you who have purchased a copy to enjoy. It takes an entire village to write a book, even more to buy and read it, and an entire planet to work together and create a better future for wildlife. Thanks for being part of this!

You Don't See This Every Day

"In zoos, as in nature, the best times to visit are sunrise and sunset. That is when most animals come to life. They stir and leave their shelter and tiptoe to the water's edge. They show their raiment. They sing their songs. They turn to each other and perform their rites. The reward for the watching eye and the listening ear is great. I spent more hours than I can count, a quiet witness to the highly mannered, manifold expressions of life that grace our planet. It is something so bright, loud, weird and delicate as to stupefy the senses."

- Pi Patel, son of a zoo director, in the book "Life of Pi" by Yann Martel

The man's hair had furrows where he had run his agitated hand. His brow had a permanent row of wrinkles, indelibly etched. Worn jeans and a casual golf shirt seemed to be a costume of the man he might have wanted to be. The hunched and hurried bearing was a dead give-away of a man who lived most of his hours in a fast-paced corporate office with a tie wrapped around his neck and a pager clipped to his belt.

Trailing behind him was a boy of about seven, wearing a bright tee shirt and shorts. A crust of ice cream was smeared on the side of his mouth, which was shaped in a perpetual expression of wonder. He had his dad's likeness — same eyes, similar sandy hair just a shade lighter — but his face was smooth-skinned and beaming with smiles, leaving no room for worry or discontent. The two brushed past me going to the butterfly exhibit. The man was head-down and heavy-footed. His son bounced and danced behind him, swiveling his head this way and that way as blooming flowers and songbirds vied for his attention.

A *"bbbrrrrrring!"* came from the man's pocket and he let go of his son's hand to pull out the cell phone and hold it to his ear. Still walking, he nodded curtly, gave terse instructions, and finished up the conversation by the time they reached the ticket-taker. His son had skipped ahead and was squatting on little haunches, breathing in the scent of an orange trumpet-vine flower that curled its tendrils on the side of the bark-chipped path. Dad signaled him back with a jerk of his chin, and the two got their hands stamped with a blurry green ink butterfly. When I, too, received my tattoo of membership, we filed through the first of two double doors.

A young ZooTeen greeted us. "Thank you for visiting the Exotic Butterfly Garden," the young lady chirped, nervously clasping her hands. She was all of 14 or 15-years old and obviously new to the job of speaking to strangers.

"Enjoy the butterflies that are flying or resting throughout this exhibit. They may alight on your clothing but please don't touch them. Touching them causes them to lose their scales that they need to fly. Also, please be careful where you put your feet because some may be resting on the bark of the path. You may need to look closely at the foliage to see some of the varieties because they are shy and their camouflage makes them blend in with leaves and flowers." She finished, out-of-breath, and hurriedly pushed open the inner door. We crowded forward to enter.

Warm, fragrant air enveloped us. A hush settled as the whistle of the zoo train, the shrill cries of peacocks, and the laughter and talk of the crowds outdoors receded. Soft bark sank under our feet as we started down the curved path, and the murmur of a small stream joined whispered voices of parents and their wide-eyed children. Clever landscaping and a wandering path made the small enclosure seem much larger. Small-leaved maples reached to the ceiling, joined by butterfly bushes with their spires of purple and white blooms. Flowering shrubs in purple, magenta, salmon, orange and yellow bloomed in profusion along the path. Wooden benches gave resting places to tired visitors and butterflies, side-by-side.

A faint whisper of wings rustled through the air and I looked up as the sun passed through some clouds. A trio of large brown-and-blue Morphos floated up towards the ceiling, turned a lazy circle, and drifted down behind a tall shrub. I headed for a bench and saw two senior citizens, beatific smiles on their faces, watching a pair of pearl-and-blue Cloaked Morningstars alight on one lady's beaded handbag. Further ahead, in the midst of a stand of waving ornamental grasses, clung a Lesser Postman with two pronounced red stripes on each wing. By the brook near a sun-warmed rock flitted a small group of Royal Blues, and a closer look showed that each blue-and-white striped wing gleamed in the dappled sun with the precision of starched military uniforms.

A Rose-of-Sharon bush lifted its glorious purple flowers to a nearby heat lamp and nectar station, and I reached out to a Painted Lady who rested there. Miraculously, she turned and fluttered onto my finger. I slowly raised her up so we could study each other, eyeball-to-eyeball. With a smile, I gently returned her to her perch on a pollen-laden pistil in the center of the flower.

Time passed by in this quiet and beautiful cathedral. The brook played its music as it burbled around smooth stones and cascaded down a low waterfall. A dozen people milled about but I felt the reverent and singular experience of communing with the Divine. For those who believe in angels, here were some painted in patterned colors more spectacular than I had ever seen.

Last week, a whole family came here to grieve their mother's death. After seeing the butterflies, they said they believed in God once again. Pi Patel says that animals *"stir and leave their shelter and tiptoe to the water's edge. They show their raiment. They sing their songs. They turn to each other and perform their rites."* I didn't hear songs or see their rites but at the water's edge, I did share gossamer moments of their silent, fluttery lives.

I turned to leave the enclosure, moving slowly and carefully so as not to disturb the blue-and-silver Spicebush Swallowtail that alighted on my hand, rolling his tongue in and out to taste remnants of pollen lingering on my thumb. A small display case was by the door, with a wooden step so that children could climb up and take a closer look. Rows of brown, tan, gray and light-green chrysalises were pinned on a board, like sets of matching coats in a closet. Each row was neatly tagged with the species, place of origin, and the date of their expected hatching. The biggest ones looked like dried brown leaves curled to form compact capsules. They were more like primitive art projects made of plant materials, than living animals impatiently waiting to hatch.

The little boy charged over, bounding up the step with a "thump" of his sneakers as he landed. He cupped his small hands above his eyes to shield his view from the glare of the mid-afternoon sun, and pressed his nose to the glass. His dad came up behind him, tolerantly amused at his son's excitement and wearing that patient look that parents cultivate in the final stretches of an outing with their kids. I stepped closer too, letting groups of people weave by me on their way to the exit doors. The earth-toned gems dangled patiently, waiting, waiting.

All of a sudden from the top row, third from the right, there was a quiver! The man caught the movement out of the corner of his eye and casually gazed back. His boy saw it too, and zeroed in on it. I crowded up close behind him, one foot on the last available space on the step, straining forward to watch. What happened next was a rapid sequence of events that pulled us all in like puppets on a string, and then yanked us back as if someone had pulled us with a fast and firm hand.

The huge brown chrysalis shivered and shook. Then it quieted, swinging slightly on the pin which held it on the board. All was silent. We held our breaths. It shook again and all of a sudden, a seam split open on the bottom of the pointed tail end! The bundle swung to a stop for a microsecond. In a flash, the seam ripped open and a furled wing erupted! A half second later, a second wing followed, and then the furred body bucked out and two antennae lashed up at attention. Six legs lurched out in quick succession, pressing mightily as they untangled and extricated themselves from their confining cell. All of a sudden, voila! BUTTERFLY!

We had all reared back when the butterfly burst out into the case, and blinked to check what we had seen. The row of chrysalises were silent and still as if an event of huge import hadn't just happened a moment ago. Like paintings in a museum they hung there, beautiful but motionless. The butterfly in question backed slowly down the board to the bottom of the case. Its curved wings were now straightening and strengthening as fluid from its core pumped into its extremities and readied it for flight.

The boy was the first to speak, with a garbled shout and exclamation. From me? Just a whoosh of breath and wide eyes. But the man was the most poignant of all. He straightened up, brushed the front of his shirt as if it had been disturbed by the drama that had unfolded before him, and said in a soft but incredulous tone: "You don't see *this* every day." His face beamed and creased with wonder, a spitting image of his son's face and countenance.

It wasn't until I was driving home sandwiched between cars in rush hour traffic, that I took time to think and reflect on this event. I felt something akin to pride that a little moment of magic at the zoo had rocked this busy corporate-type off his workplace mindset. "This is what the zoo is for," I thought, and hoped that more grown-ups had to straighten their shirts after a miracle that rumpled them during their day at the zoo.

Back at the office, the man probably had his head buried in cost-benefit analyses, income statements and shareholder reports. His daily thoughts were probably on whether the shipping schedule was on time, when that nasty legal issue would be resolved, and how the hiring was going for a key position. Whatever business he was in, his mind was probably focused on how the company could thrive and succeed. The measurement of that was the bottom line of profits. What gets him out to see the bigger picture — these miracles of birth and beauty that are fundamental to our existence and that feed us so deeply?

My mind drifted to Pi Patel once again, who said: *"I spent more hours than I can count a quiet witness to the highly mannered, manifold expressions of life that grace our planet. It is something so bright, loud, weird and delicate as to stupefy the senses."* Does that man spend enough hours in this kind of setting to truly feed and refresh his soul? Do any of us?

I neared the off-ramp to my neighborhood, breathing the evening air that rushed in through my open window as I made the lane change. I thought back to the care that went into the creation of the butterfly habitat, months before the doors even opened to zoo visitors. The focus wasn't to make it a profit center, although that is something the zoo must always be thinking about just to keep its doors open and its programs ever-improving. No, the focus was to create a balanced eco-system of beauty and magic, of observation and research, and of educational opportunities both formal and informal. In these moments of hatching, insects could make us think and feel, and ultimately inspire us to care more intensely about preserving and safeguarding the natural world around us.

Life for these butterflies start even before the eggs are laid. A curator and a keeper are assigned to oversee the exhibit, and work eight months of the year to pull off a series of standing-room-only performances that only last for the summer. Like gardeners when the first seed and plant catalogs arrive in the dead of winter, long hours are spent excitedly planning and then ordering butterflies from Costa Rica, the Tropics, and various parts of North America. Butterfly farmers, staff in other butterfly exhibits, and research journals are all consulted. Shipping schedules are arranged so enough butterflies of each type are alive and in good health at any one time, given their brief lives. Some only live 7-10 days, so countless variables need to be considered: lifespan, mortality rate, packages getting delayed in the mail, what nectar plants are available, and which butterflies will gravitate to the top, middle, or bottom of the exhibit affording every visitor a chance to see one, eye-to-eye.

The horticulture crew plans and does fieldwork through the cold and rainy winter months. Hours of thought, planning and combined experience create an environment that will be able to withstand the footsteps of thousands of people a day. On delightful sunny summer days, tourists and local visitors by the thousands will enjoy visits to the zoo. Many will follow the painted butterfly pictures on the hot asphalt and come to these doors for a peek. The landscape also needs to support the butterflies, providing a balance of food, cover, and open space so that animals can have some quiet and privacy in a natural habitat but can also be enjoyed by the viewing public. Horticulture staff and volunteers will come in each morning before the zoo is open to deadhead dying blooms, plant additional flowers so that each species has enough to eat, and prune back shrubs and trees which will grow rapidly in the warm and damp environment that is created in this small biosphere.

The Department of Agriculture's inspectors check that the tent structure and pupae hatching display are secure. Zoo staff and volunteers work diligently before and when the exhibit officially opens to be sure that no exotic butterfly escapes into the wild. Boot bottoms and pant legs of staff and visiting scientists are also watched so that hitchhikers of insects, larvae or eggs cannot make their bid for freedom outside the enclosure walls. Great care is taken to bag up all plant debris that might contain insect life, to ensure that the native insects of Oregon are not exposed to exotics that might displace them. The Japanese ladybug has already taken over the niche that supported our native ladybugs, eradicating them forever and disturbing the delicate balance that had existed in our ecosystem for millennia. We have learned from someone else's costly mistake, and take great care that not even *one* miniscule egg can roll beyond these walls.

It is a mammoth job to come up with just the right environment for the winged charges that the public comes to see. Yards of drip irrigation are mapped out and laid, trellises are designed and built, benches and bridges are constructed, stonework is laid for paths and streambeds, and a plant palette and design is created and implemented. When time grows short, an outside crew is hired to construct a large outdoor stream. Bamboo is ordered and designs are sketched out to build decorative fences and gates that direct the public to stay on the paths and to keep them safe. Rock is selected, ordered and lugged from the loading dock, to be placed with a practiced eye and a pair of strong hands. Weed cloth is laid down, gravel is spread, water is piped. The details boggle the mind.

Before the exhibit is stocked with butterflies, an astonishing amount of high-level testing, data collection and record keeping goes on. The horticulture staff constructs a stream of rocks that are carefully washed so as not to bring in eggs or adult forms of other insects. Water is piped in and is found to contain mosquito larvae a few weeks later. Inquiries are made and it is found that a gallon of bleach poured directly into the water will kill the larvae, and will evaporate within 24 hours leaving the water pure and clear for the butterflies to safely drink. Tropical plants are researched, purchased and delivered, and again, a horticulturalist's trained eye discovers that eggs of a parasitic wasp are lurking under some broad leaves.

More investigation finds a benign form of insecticidal soap that will kill the eggs but not leave residue that could damage the butterflies.

Sticky insect trap tapes are hung on plants in the enclosure and captives are counted, cataloged, recorded and assessed as to whether they will create a hazard to the butterflies the zoo has chosen to live and flourish in this space. Once the exhibit is opened and stocked, the curator, horticulture staff, and USDA continue to monitor and ensure that nothing comes out of the enclosure that can affect the native environment just outside the double doors.

Nectar plants are carefully chosen to provide nourishment for the butterflies. Host plants are avoided when possible, so insects won't have customary places to lay their eggs. Plant material found with eggs or larvae is frozen, microwaved and then incinerated, in a three-part procedure to ensure that nothing untoward escapes. Debris is then composted to be returned to the earth so new things can grow.

Records are kept about the entire process for review when plans are made for next year and the year after. More stringent criteria will be applied when needed, to nip problems in the bud. The care of the insects and education of the visitors are always uppermost on everyone's mind. Imagine if we were to take this level of social and environmental conscience and attention to detail to our corporate environment. How much natural beauty and wonder could we preserve that is now lost, polluted or irrevocably damaged? What can we learn from butterflies and blossoms that can translate to cubicles and cost savings?

I've arrived home now and pull into my own driveway. My mind wanders back to the man at the zoo as I get out of the car and push open the front door. Could his company purify the water from their building so that it is crystal clear and clean when it exits the drainpipes and heads to the river? Could they filter the exhaust so that only fresh forest air re-circulates back into our precious environment? Could they balance aesthetics, comfort and safety when designing cubicles and offices for their staff? What is their commitment to the *real* bottom line — to see their business in the context of a larger environment, rather than just a way to provide a product or service and turn a profit?

My dog prances to greet me and thumps my shins with her tail as I enter the house. As is our habit, we go directly to the garden to take a breath together and enjoy what blooms, twitters or turns golden in the waning light. She leans into me with affection and I play with her silky ears for a quiet moment or two. Dusk is gathering and the smells of dinners waft to me from neighboring houses. Squirrels scamper along my cedar fence for the last run of the day, and the sun streams through the slats of the old boards casting shadows across my lawn.

I hope the man and the boy are sitting at their own table now, telling mom what they saw today and sharing some of the miracle of a butterfly freshly hatched into this world. In a week, that particular creature will have died of old age. Others will replace it as long as dads and sons, moms and daughters, continue to see the magic of birth and beauty and fight to preserve it for generations to come. Perhaps this family will go adventuring to the zoo again, to see what other magic they can find.

I head inside to see to my own dinner. Later on, I'll pick up my copy of Life of Pi. I'll no doubt thumb through some of the dozen or more places where I've dog-eared the pages and I'll relive Pi's zoo experience. *"...a pyramid of turtles; the iridescent snout of a mandrill; the stately silence of a giraffe; the obese, yellow open mouth of a hippo; the beak-and-claw climbing of a macaw parrot up a wire fence; the greeting claps of a shoebill's bill."* These images and that of a newly hatched butterfly fuel me for the night, and for my next foray to the zoo.

Croc Talk

I was ecstatic when I found out about the volunteer program at the zoo. "Sign me up," I said, got the notebooks, took the classes, and showed up for my first try at doing an animal interpretive talk. I was so new to the ZooGuide volunteer program that my red camp shirt still smelled like starch and was sharply creased. It bunched over the thermal shirt I wore to protect me from the November chill but I wore it with pride. A temporary name badge and a pin depicting a bat were my only decorations but were my claims to fame.

The bat pin announced to those "in the know" that I had successfully given a themed talk about an animal in the African Rain Forest. I had picked the African slender-snouted crocodile. It's not that I had a particular affection for these reptiles, but I had a *decided* affection for staying warm and dry in an exhibit that was kept at a toasty 80-degrees. If I was to be an interpretive talker through the winter, I wanted to be comfortable.

Interpretive talkers are volunteers who give short talks and answer questions from the public. Visitors surveyed say that the best part of their zoo experience is when they can talk to a keeper or volunteer and learn personal anecdotes or facts about the animals. Watching animals at the zoo can be like browsing the titles of a book in a library. Unless you sit down and read a chapter or two, you don't leave with much. Interpretive talks let you stay awhile, learn what goes on behind the scenes, and get your questions answered about "How old?" "What's its name?" and "What does it eat?" The good interpretive talker also asks *you* some questions to engage your curiosity and deepen your connection with the bird, hoof stock, primate, or fish that you are now craning your neck to take a better look at.

I had designed a great speech about why the crocodiles are smiling. They are in a warm exhibit, they get fed their favorite food of fish, and they get daily health checks. My props included a model of a resin alligator on a log so it could be compared to a crocodile, a red lunchbox filled with paper picnic plates and felt cutouts of trout, and a notebook with background info on our particular crocs and other zoo animals as well. Reciting my opening line and practicing smiles and hand gestures, I strode purposefully to the doors that opened into the African Rain Forest.

I had picked a busy day for my debut. Passels of children had flooded the gates and dragged parents up and down the paths, shrieking with glee as they tried to make tigers roar and elephants trumpet. I opened the door and was met by a whoosh of warm humid air and the roar of the crowds. Kids and parents were everywhere, chattering excitedly and pressing up to the exhibits to see the animals. I eased through the throng and positioned myself in front of the glassed-in enclosure. The yellow cone proclaiming "Animal Talker" was by my side and I had a prop in each hand. It was show time!

Our massive slender-snouted crocodiles, Lance and Morgan, were hunkered down on the bottom of their pool. They were resting quietly and rising gently every 20-minutes or so to take a deep draught of air at the surface. Then they'd sink their 10-foot lengths to the bottom ever so slowly, close their lidded eyes, and smirk. Tilapia fish swam docilely around them, fairly safe from predation since the crocodiles are so well fed. Weaverbirds fluttered fancifully overhead, threading grasses into nests like ladies enjoying needlepoint over tea.

What next? Pandemonium! I hadn't experienced the trigger-fast change from the chaos of a crowd to having a wave of eager visitors engulf me. Was it the red uniform or the lifelike model I carried, or that I was someone official that they could get the inside scoop from? Kids crawled up on the carpeted benches, plucked at my sleeve, and asked: "Are they real?" "Are they dead?" "When are they gonna play?" The more impatient children announced to their playmates that "no one is in there" and marched on to see the lungfish displayed in its tank on the next level. The shyer types hid behind dad's pant leg, eyes wide, waiting for his lead to know what to look at and when to leave.

Morgan slowly slithered up and elegantly draped herself over a submerged log. Then something must have caught her fancy. Was it a weaverbird that flew too close? Perhaps a tap on the glass from a mischievous child? Or perhaps a message flashed through her reptilian brain that danger was heading her way and launched her into defensive action. Whatever the cause, Morgan heaved herself off the log, cleaved up toward the surface, and with a massive thrash of her tail, catapulted the front half of her massive body out of the water and back in with a resounding SMACK!

A horde of children rushed to the glass, pushing and shoving to get a good look. Squeals and shouts rose to a thundering din. Those looking at the turtles, snakes, and colored beetles on the upper level stampeded down the steps to take a look. I rose on my toes, clutching my resin 'gator to my chest, as kids buffeted me from all sides. I waited for the tide to subside.

The next two hours were loads of fun. I had the crowd's ear when the crocs napped, but every 20 minutes or so I'd lose their attention as it switched to the real thing. A crocodile would raise its massive head for a breath, swim a leisurely lap across the pond, or do a jaw-cracking yawn and would incite a ruckus from ecstatic kids as they gaped at those awesome rows of teeth. While we pretended to eat lunches of felt fish on paper plates, wide-eyed children debated whether Lance would chew the fish or swallow them whole. I delicately fielded questions about Lance and Morgan's gender and breeding habits and whether the pair was "married." I saw that it is indeed true that a child's attention span is next to nothing if the animal is not moving. I also saw that the more the parents get engaged, the more the kids would slow down to listen and learn.

I learned things about the crocodiles that I never knew, such as how their toenails look like the fake ones you can buy in stores and polish to a bright red. I met people from Florida who told alligator stories, and ones from Hollywood who had caimans for pets. I noticed that little boys love looking at the tail that looks like it belongs to a stegosaurus, and little girls like looking at the shiny leather squares on the reptiles' hides. I realized that being warm in November and having a place to sit is attractive to parents and grandparents, and they are inclined to linger awhile. I found out what a long answer you can get when you ask the young ones: "What is the favorite thing you've seen so far at the zoo?"

The time passed in a flash. I left only when my voice became hoarse, my throat dry, and there was a merciful pause in the action. I walked back to Volunteer Headquarters to log my hours and return my 'gator-on-a-log prop. On the way I made an emergency keeper call because an aviary bird was stuck in the branches of a tree. Then a child took a header in front of me and I charmed the boy with my felt fish and directed him and his parents to the nearest first aid station to get a band aid. Next I ran into an agitated parent and directed her to the official place to have a much-needed smoke break. Finally, I met a man who wanted to know what the zoo feeds the Arrau turtles (catfish pellets, kale, and corn, in case you're wondering). The red shirt was an invitation to connect and I was happy to interact with the crowd as I wound my way up the slope.

I was sure that the crocodiles would be remembered by the people that came my way, while perhaps the leopard, the duiker, and the gerenuk would soon be forgotten. It was the one-on-one contact with a person who knew some stories about these reptiles and knew them by name that made the difference. It was being able to touch the resin alligator to feel the difference between an alligator and crocodile snout, or to imagine what Lance and Morgan get fed each week by having "lunch" with a paper plate holding a handmade felt trout.

When I got home, I opened the closet and looked through the zoo things that I keep on the second shelf. There is a notebook of class notes, another one with animal facts, and a bulging binder with my own scribbled writings. Two animal reference books lean against a box with a lid that doesn't close any more. Inside are stacks of photos, some blurry and poorly composed but all with neatly printed descriptions and dates on the back. I sift through them and come up with a half dozen shots of Lance and Morgan. They paddle towards me, studiously ignore me, or glower ominously with their steady gaze and toothy grins. I admire them, respect them, and am getting to know them, one day at a time.

Next week I'm back at the zoo for another croc talk. It'll undoubtedly be cold and rainy but I'll head to a place that's warm with smiles, laughter, and two fascinating crocodiles. Perhaps I'll see you there?

Connecting with the Creatures

Enter a zoological garden with wild animals from far away lands — what a dazzling experience! Where else can you be nose-to-nose with intriguing creatures from the far reaches of our planet? I can squat by the glass to get up close and personal with an orangutan that is pulling a burlap sack over her head. It's Inji, and she's playing a light-hearted game of peek-a-boo with Batik, the other female who ducks behind a nearby branch. I lean over the railing and watch Damara zebras grazing in the afternoon sun. They remind me of Uncle Jim's horses wearing black-and-white pajamas and I notice for the first time that even their hooves are striped!

I'll probably go to the indoor elephant viewing area, too. One of the elephant cows cuddles a younger female by curling her trunk and brushing the calf's neck and sides as the little one sleeps between those massive feet. And do I have time for a ride on the train? I walk that way and am might be startled by a hiss and a scream as the Amur tigers spar and tumble with each other on the ledge above.

I am pulled to the zoo again and again, for meaningful personal encounters and connections. As a writer, I train myself daily to observe and think, to listen to others and to peer from behind the lens of their unique perspectives. It's not a conclusion I am after, but rather a collection of new ways to connect with these animals. I can have my zoo visit be a deeper exploration rather than just entertainment on a Sunday afternoon. Nowhere in your daily routine are you faced with such diversity of life. How does the average zoo-goer make sense of all this? How do we connect with these creatures?

I came to the zoo one day with no other goal than to wonder and wander — to enjoy myself. This was my time for connecting with the creatures. I tagged along behind a group of moms pushing strollers and we wound along the path. The chimps roamed around their large grassy enclosure and were being sketched by a pair of industrious teens. Smudged fingers, knitted brows, and the flow of ink on 80# Bristol drew us all to tiptoe in and take a closer look. Bright eyes stared back from a tangle of fur, and a nose was born with deft sweeps of pen on paper.

I thought back to a figure drawing class I took where the textbook had a series of human noses of all different kinds. I was astounded to see how much variety there was and all were from the same species, *Homo sapiens*. Among our human friends we see big ones, little ones, crooked ones, pug ones. In the zoo this range is multiplied by 200 different species! We see black rubbery noses with flaring nostrils; hard bills of varying shapes and sizes with nose-holes on the ends; long prehensile trunks that drink water, make sounds, and pick up food; and smelling centers on the roof of reptilian mouths that sense particles in the air that their forked tongues draw in. Some days I scratch my head in awe. Other times, I just accept the beauty that comes in so many unexpected packages.

In either case, our neural pathways all respond in a similar way. Human brains are hard-wired to receive a new experience like watching a DeBrazza monkey for the first time, and immediately sift through their memory banks to find something similar. Debra, the female DeBrazza, is a patchwork-quilt sort of primate. Her body looks like a chinchilla with soft gray fur and subtle highlights. The white patch on her chest reminds me of our neighborhood cat. The orange-colored fur around her head reminds me of the golden lion tamarin I saw earlier in the day. The button nose reminds me of a teddy bear I have tucked away in my guest room closet. My mind puts these disparate parts together and burns a new neuron pathway that I can now access and recall as "DeBrazza monkey." I now have a new connection with a creature.

Past the classrooms is the Malayan sun bear exhibit. Jody and Vivian drape themselves in a jumble of fabricated tree branches, soaking in the feeble rays of wintery sun through their dark coats. Their nostrils flare as a breeze sends the fragrance of freshly made waffle cones from the nearby concession stand. Some of their branches are real and some are gunnite reinforced with rebar and wire mesh, but the popular crotches are those with heating units in them that provide a cozy place to nap.

Kids are trying to clamber up on the metal railing so they can get a closer look at these "honey bears" and I'm jostling for room so I can see too. The animals look like the bear in their favorite Winnie the Pooh book. Kids will often try to compare the animal to something they already know. One of the most commonly asked questions of keepers during the keeper talks is: "How old is it?" It's an attempt to relate their life to the bear's in a fundamental way. Some children will go on to ask if it is a boy or girl bear, and often the small children will ask if they have any babies. What better way to relate to an animal than to find one just like themselves, that is cute, funny, and tumbling around to explore so many things for the very first time?

When the toddlers are nose-to-nose with a baby animal, isn't the next level of wondering to ask what the animal's name is? To name something is to know it, and they can feel a connection when they can talk about an animal as if it's a friend. It is a proven fact that the way to instill a sense of connection and stewardship in children is to expose them when they're young.

Bring four to seven year olds to the zoo and they begin to develop empathy with the natural world. They like baby animals and feel their pain if the animals are hungry or separated from their mothers. They like to imitate animals and run like the giraffes or jump like the tigers. Kids will race by an exhibit if there is no action or baby animals, but take them to the Allen swamp monkey exhibit where twins are riding on the backs of their monkey-mom and the kids are glued to the glass, absorbed and connected.

By the elementary school years, children are no longer only focused on what's going on at home but want to explore further afield. This exploration drives them to go out and interact with their environment. These are the kids that are climbing over guard rails to play in the foliage, tapping on the glass to wake up the slumbering sloth, and throwing leaves and twigs into the ponds and streams of the exhibits to see what they can stir up. They are also first in line to touch the horns on a giraffe skull or feel the fur on a lion pelt. The more adventurous will even stroke the scales of a live boa constrictor! They are tactile and interactive, and their energy to seek out these connections is boundless.

By early adolescence, the 12 to 15-year olds are ready to take on the world. They can read the maps and understand that these animals are from Africa, Asia or the Arctic. It is also the first time that they realize they can have a role in conservation efforts to preserve the mighty condors and bald eagles. Before this age, telling children about endangered species, habitat loss, and why some animals can never be released back into the wild, paints a sobering picture that young ones aren't ready to shoulder. Children don't want to be sent out into a world that is flawed or spoiled before they have a sense that they can actually do something about it. These older kids are empowered with information and fueled by an innate curiosity. They begin to explore perspectives and lifestyles like recycling, vegetarianism and social action. They connect in a powerful way. The zoo introduces critical conservation issues being debated out in the world and these children now see themselves as part of the solution.

I get a kick out of the adults, too. Our celebrated Asian elephant, Packy, was born in 1962 when I was still in diapers. Other Portlanders were too, and in my hours hanging around the elephant barn, I'm constantly amazed at how proprietary people are about him and how they have followed the events of his life over the decades. His birthday in April is celebrated with a gargantuan cake and lots of hoopla, a mural of him graces a prominent downtown building, and he has developed quite an entourage of fans who call him by name. They pay attention when they hear him ramming his head against the metal doors in hopes that the keepers will give him food to quiet him. "Why isn't he fed enough?" they demand. They show him off to relatives and scour the gift shop for postcards of his likeness. A visit to the zoo is not complete without paying their respects to him.

When Pet, an elderly female elephant, cocks a foot to take the weight off it, zoo visitors who know her can almost *feel* the arthritic pain that a gargantuan daily dose of ibuprofen can hardly take the edge off. She is receiving exceptional medical care yet her fans press forward with questions and want status reports. They have connected with this elephant herd. If one of the elephants were pregnant, dozens of fans in Portland would no doubt be feeling false labor pains! In the early 1960's, children had a massive penny drive and collected enough funds to bring Rose-Tu to the zoo. I think this is great. Strong connections build a strong community. I feel warm and fuzzy when it includes the animals of the zoo and heartfelt care about their well-being.

This same impulse to connect has people signing up in droves to be ZooParents. For a modest fee, you can adopt an animal such as one of the mountain goats at Cascade Crest. For your donation you get a photograph, information on mountain goats, and a newsletter keeping you abreast of related zoo news. Interspecies-adoptions are not real in the sense that you are not responsible for the care, feeding and rearing of your animal. Still, I bet I'll find you lingering by the ledges and gunnite snow-fields of the habitat keeping track of mom, dad, and the kid as a required stop when you visit the zoo; scanning for photos and articles about them in the zoo newsletter and on the website; and talking importantly to perfect strangers who come up behind you to explain what's going on with *your* goats! Where will *you* find *me*? Grinning like a fool at Debra, our DeBrazza monkey, because I'm her ZooParent and feel like a delinquent parent if a foray to the zoo doesn't include visiting her.

The renovated refreshment stand now houses the intriguing creatures of the Insect Zoo. I wonder, how do we connect with animals that are not furry and warm for cuddling? It's easy to relate to a primate like the chimpanzee since it looks like a little humanoid, is playful, seems non-threatening, and is as familiar to us as one of the stock zoo animals. But what happens when we look through the glass and see an Australian walking stick? This is an enormous insect, thick and juicy, with magnificent insect mandibles that chomp through a blackberry leaf with the precision of a chainsaw. It's creepy and crawly and would send shivers up the spine of most of us if one scuttled across our palm. The only thing we have in common with it is a love of summer blackberries and even here, they prefer the leaves while we prefer the berries.

I press my face close to the glass and peer into the tank that is humming with six-legged life. Not only are there more species of insects than any other animal on our planet, but by sheer weight and volume, insects have more mass than all the animals alive today. In addition, insects have a bigger impact on our daily lives than the large exotics that we are prone to worry about as their names are added one by one to the endangered species list. Yes, the lions, tigers and bears are important, but without insects to pollinate crops and feed birds and break down detritus in our forests, life as we know it would grind to a halt. They are the bottom of the food chain and as such, are fundamental to all the life that comes above them. Antennae wave and beady eyes peer up at me, and I mouth to them a silent "thanks."

Our insect zoo is gleefully staffed by teen volunteers in the summer. They'll let you gawk at the walking stick, stand inches away from a hissing cockroach, or tell you how the centipede mother makes a nest in the forest floor and guards her eggs. Mothers, fathers, don't be shy. Why should the kids have all the fun? Push on forward and brace yourself for the feeling of six slender legs tap dancing on your palm, or a hard body scuttling across your fingers. Touch them, admire them, and understand their importance. Drag your spouse forward to have a peek. This experience times ten thousand other peoples' will ultimately lead to support and funding for the conservation efforts and research that are critical to the preservation of our planet.

How can we muster up the caring that is needed to protect life, all life, whether it is a DeBrazza monkey, Malayan sunbear, Asian elephant, mountain goat, or

Australian walking stick? I take a last look at the walking stick that is munching contentedly on a blackberry leaf, and turn to head home for the day. I don't have to solve all the problems of the world, nor even answer all the questions that the zoo brings up for me today. Instead, I can continue to wonder and wander. Michael Ventura, author of <u>The Zoo Where You're Fed to God</u>, puts it quite well. He, too, has spent many hours wondering and wandering around a zoo.

> *"I'm beginning to think of the zoo as a center, a node, out of which radiates the unthinkable solitude of the bison, the unwavering watchfulness of the tiger, the sweet dignity of the giraffe, the playful tenderness of the chimpanzee, the delicacy of the gerenuk, the stillness of the jaguar — radiating out in waves upon the city, like fountains of spirit, from which all drink without knowing, and to which people take their children not to see but to drink, to drink from this stream to replenish what is being lost: solitude and watchfulness, tenderness, dignity and delicacy, stillness and sweetness – here, where the world is ending, they are in plenty."*

I like the beauty of his words, and hope that people spend time at the zoo so they can soak in these "fountains of spirit" and in turn, feel connected to the creatures.

Proud Tigers and Lonely Bears

Mikhail hauls his striped length out of the pool and lashes his rope of a tail, sending a spray of water droplets on Nicole's back. She scrambles up, startled awake from her nap. She pads over to Mikhail and they brush whiskers before turning and going their separate ways. He turns his attention back to the pool and the plastic bucket that he was playing with, and she wanders off to find a quieter place to resume her nap.

I watch these tigers a lot. Most of the time they are sleeping, but sometimes they swim, play, roar, or stalk imaginary prey inside their exhibit. I recall what Jeffrey Moussaieff Masson and Susan McCarthy wrote in a classic book called: <u>When Elephants Weep: The Emotional Lives of Animals</u>. Discussing circus animals, they say:

> "Some captive animals experience little joy in life. For some, performing may be a chance to

> work, to display prowess, to feel proud. A tiger who cannot hunt, cannot mate with other tigers, and cannot explore and survey its territory has little chance of feeling pride."

Sure, I want tigers to feel joy, to have work, to show what they can do, and to feel proud because that's what I want in my life. But what yearnings actually live inside their graceful bodies? What longings are reflected in their golden gaze?

Let's travel back to the wilds and see what the tiger's natural life is really like. He snoozes more than 80% of his life, digesting his kill and resting up for the next hunt. When he's hungry, he prowls for food. When he kills and eats, he's satiated. Quite frankly, I don't think he cares who sees his prowess. He just wants to get the job done. And feeling proud? I'd wager that a tiger just wants to quiet the gnaw of hunger by feasting, and then take a long digestive nap in the sun.

If a captive tiger cannot hunt but gets three squares a day, is that so bad? If he gets enrichment activities that stimulate his hunting instincts and a companion to lie on a ledge with, he may not feel pride but he can have many moments of contentment in between his many naps. If his companion is too old or not to his liking, fights would erupt, they would be separated, and the tigers would not breed. We may want a cub each year as regular as clockwork, but in the wild, tigers breed when circumstances are right and probably don't brood over it when they're not. They don't feel inferior or brood about their self-esteem issues if they can't "get lucky" or feel like their life didn't play out correctly if they can't leave progeny behind.

As humans, we are a complex lot. We can be plagued by cycling emotions, jubilations of the highest order, unmet needs that gnaw at us, overwhelming responsibilities that settle on our shoulders, and despair that can give way to inspiration and focused action, all in the same day! It is a given, then, that as we go through the gates of the zoo, we bring our feelings with us.

One feeling is loneliness. I mosey over to the café for some hot cocoa and peer down into the aviary as I sip my warm drink. Families and couples crowd the tables around me but I am alone. I rarely feel lonely, yet on occasion, a raw feeling steals over me and points out that I have no toddler by my side nor husband waiting at home to hear of my adventures at the zoo. Today, there's no one to nudge in the ribs and point as the musk ox takes a dip in the pond, and no one to smile at as an otter sucks on her tail as she settles down to her nap.

Loneliness… we've all experienced it. In the short, cold, wet, gray days of winter your grandmother holes up at home with only the TV for company. Maybe your teen-aged daughter is listless, saddened by the loss of her first love. The neighbor across the way has time on his hands, because the plant laid off workers and he hasn't found another job yet. Your best friend spends more time in airplanes and at hotels than in her own home, and calls every night from the road just to hear a familiar voice.

At these times of disconnection we long for the warmth and company of another. What about you? You might head for the zoo on just such a day, or even become a volunteer because you have an affection for anything with feathers or fur. It is inevitable that you'll project feelings onto the animals you see. It's like when you're in love, every song on the country music station is celebrating with you — dancing, making love, and planning the perfect family. When you break up, all of a sudden that same country station has nothing but cowboys who have lost their truck, their horse, and their woman, and are halfway through their second six-pack! It's hard to separate our personal feelings from what we see out in the world, and there's no better place to explore this phenomenon than at the zoo.

If you're peering in the exhibits when you're feeling down, you'll probably ask yourself: "Do animals feel lonely too?" I asked that question myself, as I chatted with a keeper in the Arctic Tundra area. He told me a great story. One Christmas day, there was a celebration in the grizzly bear barn at the Denver Zoo. Triplets were born! Amidst toasts and slaps on the back, zoo staff created records for the tiny cubs and stopped, pens poised at the blank that said "Name." In the spirit of the holidays and with a sly humor, one keeper probably spoke his suggestion in jest: "Bah Humbug!" Whatever the actual story, the three little bears were nicknamed Bah, Hum, and Bug amidst the cheers of the holiday crowd. The names that were actually put down in the book were strong sturdy names that came from mountains in the area. McKinley and Denali ended up at the Oregon Zoo. The unspoken understanding at our zoo is that animals are given names appropriate to their homeland or respectful of their character or personality, rather than cute or trite names that make fun of animals or put them in the category of a house pet.

The lone female went adventuring to live in a zoo far away in South Dakota. The two males came here to Oregon. McKinley grew big and strong and lived a couple of decades before he died of cancer. Denali resides here to this day and entertains hundreds of youngsters and oldsters alike, every day. But we've got to wonder, isn't this great bruin lonely?

When we hear the story, our hearts seize up with sadness. Triplets, separated from each other! We might blink back damp eyes thinking of poor McKinley, dying without both his siblings there to provide comfort and hold his paw. We then turn to outrage — sending the female so far away from her brothers! And then we turn our gaze to the solitary grizzly who sits chest deep in the pond and catches apple chunks that Carl, his keeper, tosses to him. We look into his deep brown eyes and think we see a little quiver there, a haunting sadness. The poor little fellow. Even though he is 550 pounds of solid muscle and a daunting presence of power and might, our hearts go out to him and his fragile emotions. We need a hug so we want to make sure all the bears get their apportionment, whether the bear thinks he needs one or not. We'd like nothing better than to hike up through his 3-acre exhibit and slip our arms around his girth, giving him the comfort we long for ourselves. We restrain ourselves, however. His claws are built for digging tubers and stripping branches and he'd make short work of us if we ventured into his territory.

We might also want to restrain ourselves from anthropomorphizing — interpreting what is not human in terms of human or personal characteristics. This is the thinking that goes on a lot, as we work our way around the zoo. We can't help it, because we're trying to connect with the animals. Why is this one in such a small cage? Quite possibly, he has arthritis and can't move around much. He might even need a small territory that he feels confident guarding, therefore feeding and breeding better than if placed in a larger enclosure. Why is this other one so lethargic? Maybe because it's time for her mid-morning nap. Or maybe she's very old. Why are they pacing? Maybe because enrichment scents have just been introduced to their enclosure and they are deciding whether to go hunting or not, or they are hearing the keeper in the kitchen fixing snacks and are impatient. Maybe they are indeed bored. Have you ever asked a child how often they are bored in a single day? If it's once or a half dozen times, that is still par for the course and acceptable in my mind for a fine and fulfilling life.

We could explore this further by finding a diverse group of zoo goers and asking each one what they thought of the behavior of a particular group of primates. A child thinks he is bored. A single mom points out the lack of mates for each animal. An adolescent views the enclosure as restrictive and closed in. An elderly person notices the comfortable sleeping nests and climate controlled heating and cooling for the animals' comfort. A lonely young adult thinks the group is too small. An over-worked office manager thinks there's not enough privacy. An engineer questions the thickness of supports and the strength of the mesh. A psychologist questions how often enrichment activities are provided. One person may see the animals as helpless victims. Another might appreciate the opportunities of a protected life at the zoo. It's clear that there are a whole range of perspectives, none of which might be totally accurate.

Anthropomorphizing is a common practice but when we look deeper at these animals and their ways with a bit of neutrality, we can learn a lot. Take grizzlies, for instance. It's counter-adaptive for them to share territory so they are usually solitary in the wild. There's only one bear for a vast expanse of forest and mountain. They rarely run into one another. If the truth were known, they don't *want* to visit with each other. Berry picking and hunting down small game is fine done alone. When they seek each other out, it's for breeding. When the female mates, delivers her cubs, and raises them, it is a two- to three-year process to teach the cubs survival skills. Does she get lonely for her mate? Nah. It's tough enough to find food for herself and the hungry mouths of her growing cubs. Having her mate around would be nothing but competition for existing food sources. We cannot expect that adult bears like to take long walks through the moonlit forest, making plans for the next romantic interlude and the next batch of cubs they are planning for the future. It's just not like that with this species. They, like many other animals, play out most of the dramas and contentments of their lives in singular bliss.

We can do laps around the zoo poking our noses and projecting our psyches into cages, tanks and enclosures. But we will stretch our empathy to the limit if we don't step back and take a good look from the other side of the bars. What does each individual animal truly need for a good life, in or out of a zoo?

I've circled back to Mikhail and Nicole in the tiger exhibit. Mikhail rolls on his back and gives it a luxurious scratch against the heated rock that he often naps on. I can't see Nicole at first but then I spot her. She is lurking among tall grasses by the trees, watching one of our free-range peacocks with an intent look. I suppose Denali is doing grizzly things like uprooting logs in search of enrichment treats, paddling in the pond to cool off, or listening to the kids howl to the wolves next door. I leave them to their lives and head up to the exit gate, living my own sometimes proud and hardly ever lonely existence.

Wapiti Wisdom

On Fridays I punch out the combination on the heavy staff gate, shoulder it open, and enter the world of foliage, soil and irrigation in my job as a horticulture volunteer. I typically spend time in bamboo thickets cutting browse for the elephants, and then might be on my knees in the cool loam of the elephant overlook planting sword ferns, or hip-deep in a tangle of thickets in the upper viewing area cutting it down to size. As a hands-on volunteer with a weekly shift, I get to be intimately connected to a small section of the zoo. It's a nice feeling. In a world that can be overwhelming in its demands, I like puttering around in just a small corner of Eden.

Today, I'm just a looker, not a doer. I wear a tank top, shorts and sandals rather than gardening clothes, boots and gloves. I bring nothing but a camera slung around my neck, and bottled water for a thirst that is already building under the hot summer sun. It's great to be here at the zoo as a visitor for the first time in months. I am eager to go exploring....

I stroll down the ramp and wander to the amphitheater to see what's going on. I watch a presenter on stage with an enormous condor, answering questions from an eager summer crowd of sun-tanned children. In the Alaska Tundra exhibit, I press forward with a family that peppers the grizzly bear keeper with questions about his hefty charge and watch as he feeds the bear some apple chunks. I wander through the butterfly exhibit with other open-mouthed visitors and see rainbow shades of swallowtails, monarchs and buckeyes drift dreamily through the blooms and branches of their fragrant enclosure.

Finally, I make my way to the Northwest section with the hopes of hearing a keeper speak about the elk. It's an area off the beaten path, and I have not been here before. I am way too early, so I am given the gift of a half hour of quiet waiting and watching as only a handful of other zoo visitors come and go. The male elk rests in regal splendor before me, thoughtfully chewing his cud and balancing a huge rack of antlers on his brow.

The elk is called the wapiti by the native people of Spirit Lake. The educational sign says mankind used the hide for clothing and drums, antlers for weapons and digging tools, meat for sustenance, and spirit for the sacred stories. This type of species identification is an "old school" zoo approach, where animals are defined by what they can provide for man. I am curious about this narrow description that only covers this animal's usefulness to us. The logical question to follow is: "What is the usefulness of *Homo sapiens*?"

I wrinkle my forehead and search for answers as I cross the viewing deck to get a look at the small herd. Women can provide breast milk for our own or others' young. We can provide locks of hair for those who are left bald by chemotherapy or organs if we carry our official donor card. I am hard pressed to find anything useful about our hides and we are sorely lacking in antlers. Our spirit could be used for sacred stories but have we really benefited the global ecosystem in any way or have we just rearranged it? It makes me wonder who is the greater of the species, wapiti or us? Who should be in the enclosure, and who should be required to provide "useful things?"

The planks squeak beneath my feet as I stroll to the next education plaque. By pressing buttons we can hear a mating call, a fighting match between two wapiti bulls, and the call of a mother to her calf. Kids press them and jump back, alarmed and then fascinated by the bellows and barks and cries that come from the loudspeaker. After a dozen rounds of these antics, I sort through a comparison of the wapiti life cycle to ours. Finding food, seeking a mate, and protecting our young are our common denominators. What if humans could focus on doing those things extraordinarily well? If we pulled in all those resources that fly us to Mars or design running shoes with interactive microchips and stick to the basics, wouldn't our civilization be healthier, happier and more self-secure? Instead, we can be derailed by other things like religious piousness without heart, trophy houses that aren't homes, and big bank accounts that focus more of our attention on the vagaries of the stock market than on understanding and accepting the cycles of our own bodies as they mature and age. Wise men have often said that nature's laws are the only ones that uniformly govern all who live on this planet. If it works for the wapiti, why shouldn't it work for us? The wapiti offers us some clear lessons in the simplicity of its undomesticated life.

I watch the lone wapiti in his spot in the shade. He has his back to us on the viewing platform, studiously ignoring the train as it makes the curve by the enclosure and toots its whistle. He is unblinking when recordings of his long lost cousins call to a mate, fight with another bull, or call to their calf. He chews his cud rhythmically because that is what wapiti do in the mid-afternoon when it is too hot to be standing in the middle of the sunny meadow. He faces a chain link fence and doesn't try to break out, but accepts his fate of being enclosed in a relatively small space. There is a calm peace in him, and an elegance and majesty with his huge rack of antlers, as he contemplates Buddha-like on the grass.

I cannot imagine what he's thinking but perhaps he takes the "long view." He finds comfort in regular food and shelter, enjoys the company of the two elk cows that share the habitat, accepts the rain as a natural companion to the sun, and doesn't sweat the small stuff. Perhaps our fascination with animals is that we can see our own lives in theirs. The parallel in my life is clear to me. I should accept where I am and be fully present there, and play out the fullest expression of my nature much as the wapiti does in his share of space at the zoo. The native peoples looked to the elk as a great and wise teacher. I can too. We understand only a thin layer of what makes up their life, yet that understanding can take us deep into the layers of our own complex social and psychological matrix and somehow lead us to insight and learning.

One of the great strengths of elk is their ability to sustain a trot for long distances. It's their predominant defense against predators because they can simply outrun them. How can I hit my own stride? What areas of life call to me for extra effort, more staying power, and the ability just to hang in there and keep working on a project, a relationship, or on weathering a rough patch with health or general happiness? It takes years for an elk to reach maturity, to develop those huge haunch muscles that propel it forward, and to grow a heart that is big and strong enough to serve its body when it runs. Can I develop that same patience as I invest time in my writing projects or my relationships? If I slow my gallop to a steady trot and use the wapiti as my benchmark, perhaps I can craft a life of my own making that has as its watchword a self-renewing pace.

Elk are communal creatures and look out for one another. They usually have "watchouts" where certain elk will sound the alarm by bugling or will raise and reveal a large rump patch for all to see as a danger warning. The young are targets for predators so elk are extremely protective. Mature females will often take charge of the group's young while other females wander for food, and use their sharp hooves if danger threatens. What community do *I* live in? What would I do for my extended family if danger threatened? Do I know my neighbors by name? Do I have enough friends to feel like I live in a tribe of kindred souls? If my young are threatened, do I understand the threat and can I fight back? Community is basic yet sometimes overlooked until there is a reason to circle the wagons and huddle within that protection. It is only then that we think about danger and friends, and the place of both in our world.

The two cows have meandered over and lie together under a stand of trees. They chew their cud and slowly blink their long eyelashes. Their slow, steady breathing is restful to watch. I find my eyes getting heavy as I watch them relax in the sun. My breathing slows too. I find my thoughts emptying and my body filling with a warm and comforting peace. I've spent many hours on a meditation cushion throughout my life. It's a difficult discipline because we define ourselves by action, not by contemplation or rest. Still, in all my seeking to understand my life and how to live it, it is in silence with my breath that I return home to a place where all is balanced, all is well. I'm not an herbivore and have no reason to re-chew my food, but I can sit in meditation or with a cup of tea, to enjoy the simple pleasures of taking in sustenance in a slow and mindful way.

I rise from the bench, with one last look at the massive bull elk with the velvet-covered antlers. The keeper has not come to tell us about making drums of wapiti hide or how to use the bones and antlers as weapons. I am glad, because I have pondered deeper questions and received great wisdom from this magnificent creature. I can question being defined by my usefulness to myself or others. I can see the rightness of a satisfying life of simple living, good food, good loving, friends and family. I can try to play out my animal nature and fully express myself, free from mental or societal constraints. And finally, I can rest easy where I am right here, right now, in this calm, quiet moment of my existence.

Care of the Long-Necks

The shadows grow long as dusk begins to settle gently upon the zoo. Visitors follow exit arrows, streaming towards waiting cars with sleepy children in tow. As the crowd thins, a quietness and stillness settles even as the heat rises up from the still-hot pavement. Leaves rustle gently in the trees. Songbirds come out to feed on evening insects and send ribbons of music through the Rose-of-Sharon shrubs on which they perch.

I am still at my post at the giraffe exhibit, where I parked myself hours ago to view *Giraffa camelopardalis reticulata*. I came here to watch one animal for an extended period of time, and to hear what the visitors had to say when they first caught sight of these magnificent creatures. It thrills me to see faces light up and tired steps quicken their pace as people rush to the railing to gawk. No one has come for a while though, and I will need to go soon before security guards do the final sweep to ensure that everyone has gone. Still, I linger just a moment longer to sniff the faintly horse-like smell of giraffe, listen to the methodical chomp-chomp-chomp of alfalfa being masticated by walnut-sized molars, and look deep into the brown eyes of Akeem, the male reticulated giraffe.

Akeem is just out of reach, but I am closer to a giraffe than I'll probably ever be in my lifetime. The pointy protuberances on his head and his cartoon-like snout make me think of dinosaurs. The impression is reinforced by the fact that he is absolutely HUGE! Never mind the delicate legs, long eyelashes and wispy tail. This creature weighs about 2000 pounds and is enormously tall — over 16 feet, which is the height of three men standing on each other's shoulders! For safety's sake, the visitors look down on Akeem and his sunken enclosure from a wooden platform. This way we can get a look at his head and see him eye-to-eye rather than crane our necks to stare at about 10-feet of legs and underbelly. Still, his height and presence are awe-inspiring from whatever vantage point we look and from wherever we wonder.

The giraffe is a favorite of many zoo-goers because of its beauty, grace and power. In Paris, the French had a particular attraction to this animal almost 200 years ago! Vicki Croke writes about the first giraffe shipped to France in her book <u>The Modern Ark</u>:

> "A beautiful female left Alexandria in 1826 aboard an Italian brigantine, with her every comfort cared for. She had a room cushioned with straw, an ocean view from a shaded window, a Muslim medal around her neck to keep her safe, three Sudanese keepers and three cows to provide twenty-five liters of milk a day. She wintered in Marseilles, rejecting many of the meals adoringly presented to her, consuming mostly milk and maize-and-barley porridge. Life was a whirl of formal parties and, in nicer weather, elaborate parades with her retinue of three cows reassuringly at her side. A poncho and hood were sewn for her 500-mile journey to Paris."

Croke goes on to give us details about this pampered giraffe's actual trip:

> "It took two months for this elegant ungulate to make the trip on foot and all along the way, crowds lined the streets, dazzled by her exotic beauty. King Charles himself fed the regal animal rose petals from his hand. Hundreds of Parisians came to see her and a cottage industry of giraffe goods grew — giraffe soaps, cake molds, paperweights, toys, ointments, wallpaper, parasols and toothpick holders among them."

I find it hard to relate that animal's experience with that of Akeem and his pal, J.C. in the naturalistic exhibit at the Oregon Zoo. I would rather see them here or in the wilds of sub-Saharan Africa, where they can go about their giraffe-like business unburdened by medals, ponchos, and maize-and-barley porridge. We are not in the "wilds," but I like to squint my eyes into the setting sun and have the barriers between us seem to disappear.

In that golden blur and the quiet of the evening, I take a moment and close my eyes to smell, listen, and imagine what it's like to be a giraffe — to splay those long legs to reach the ground, ever wary for predators that might attack; to roam the enclosure looking for nibbles up high where bamboo and tropical foliage dangle just out of reach; to be surrounded by the quiet hush of forest and the swish of irrigation sprinklers on one side, and the ever-changing raucous palette of zoo visitors on another; to be downwind from intriguing scents of hippos, monkeys, cranes and kudus, and to occasionally get the whiff of tiger danger or leopard hunger from points further away; and to have the noise of traffic on Highway 26 and the occasional plane that comes in for a landing at the airport just 15 miles to the northeast. What a different experience from a pampered giraffe visiting Paris, or of native animals on the open savannah of Africa!

The quiet also leads me to daydream and imagine. What would someone from 100 years ago say, if he or she could walk down these paths on a late summer evening? Would they approve of how we care for these long-neck wonders? My eyes drift shut and I slouch comfortably on a donor bench overlooking the feeding station. Moments pass and I dream, pleasantly tired from my day and lost in my imaginings. I am in that fog between sleep and awakening when on the path to my left, I hear the steps of someone approaching. The person moves slowly and quietly, taking his time as he comes up to the exhibit. I am surprised to see a diminutive bespectacled man in bare feet, wearing an off-white robe. Imagine my surprise to see that he looks like Mahatma Gandhi himself! Before I can sit up and acknowledge his presence, he rearranges his dhoti, takes a quiet look at me, and then peers over to watch Akeem and J.C. pull strands of alfalfa from the feeder.

"I have looked at your zoo. I have read your educational information. I have seen your exhibits," he says quietly. He gives me another thoughtful look. He then voices a sentiment that has been widely quoted: "We can judge the greatness of a nation by the way it treats its animals."

He folds his hands quietly on the railing, looks straight ahead, and takes a deep breath of the still summer evening. Slow and groggy from my little nap, it takes me a few moments to let the words catch up with me and to collect my thoughts. Then they start spinning, as I race through what little I know about the history of zoos. It all started many lifetimes ago, when we first brought animals into captivity....

The scent of incense is in the air and the rustle of stiff cloth comes from behind me. In the darkening shade of the nearby trees, I see a woman approaching. Oh my gosh, it's Queen Hatshepsut! It wasn't a man but a woman who launched the first animal collecting expedition in 1490 B.C.. She comes nearer, spies me on the bench, and narrows her kohl-rimmed eyes as she speaks. "I would like one of these," she announces with a commanding tone, nodding towards the pair of giraffes. I guess she got one, because a bas-relief of this elegant animal still exists and it was probably the first giraffe ever seen in Egypt.

Queen Hatshepsut is soon joined by a Chinese man in a flowing robe and I immediately recognize him as Emperor Wen of the Zhou dynasty. He set up the Garden of Intelligence around 1100 B.C.. It was probably a hunting park but the belief of the time was that animals were the communication link between humans and the spiritual realms. He has never seen a giraffe before but I can tell his brain is working feverishly, while his hands are clasped in meditative prayer. Was he thinking what fun it would be to hunt and kill a specimen like this, or was he thinking loftier thoughts about its spiritual connection? With such a long neck, shouldn't a giraffe be able to access high levels of information and provide a far-reaching perspective for the common man?

The Egyptian queen and the Chinese emperor move off, and I scrub my eyes to wake up from this strange dream. A noise startles me from further along the path and with quite a commotion, a royal family from ancient Assyria gathers before me. Semiramis, a 9th century B.C. courtesan, is searching for leopards. Her son, Ninus, looks for lions for their collection. These animals are further down so I point to the directional arrows and send them on their way. The Assyrians were quite amazing collectors and importers of exotic animals, and by the 4th century B.C., animal collections were a part of ancient Grecian civilization and fueled an interest in the study of zoology.

I hear a commotion that turns my head. A fistfight ensues and I jump up to see what the ruckus is about. A swarthy man in a toga looks to be the instigator. When I question him, he belligerently says he is Marcus Fulvius Nobilitor. "I am here to find animals for The Games," he proclaims, and those around him hiss in disapproval. Gandhi serenely leaves our bench, steps in, and quiets the group. I retreat to safety behind a nearby shrub. I recall that Marcus, Octavius, Nero and others collected animals to fight in battle or for sport in arenas.

The whole pack marches off, sullen but quiet, and Gandhi and I are left with the peaceful evening once again. He begins to talk about history and I avidly listen. It seems that mankind went back and forth for a while in the treatment of animals. As Gandhi said, how they viewed and treated animals tells us much about their culture. Constantine put an end to the slaughter of collecting animals for hunting, war, and fighting matches, but Justinian brought bloodshed back. In the Dark Ages, wild animal collections were scaled down and cared for by royal families or monks in monasteries. Perhaps it was here that people began collecting animals for the love of them, rather than to use them for sport or prestige.

Charlemagne was another well-known animal lover and then zoos diminished in popularity until Frederick II revived the idea again. And so it went, with influential figures like Henry III, Marco Polo, Cheng Tzu, and Columbus having a hand in keeping captive exotic animals. Lorenzo de' Medici had an intriguing story in 1487. He promised the gift of a giraffe to Louis XI's daughter in exchange for the release the sultan of Egypt's brother who was being held captive in France. The giraffe was never delivered, causing no end of international intrigue.

The stories went on and on, but light was fading and time was passing. I was interested in talking with some more contemporary personalities, because I was intrigued with Gandhi's notion of how cultural values and attitudes about stewardship of animals show up in zoos. Gandhi looked a bit parched so I sent him off to get himself some tea. He turned the corner and wandered curiously towards the concessions stand where the smell of freshly baked waffle cones lingered in the air.

But now, look who's here! Around the far bend I see a man in wool coat and hat. It is Carl Hagenbeck, an animal supplier and showman from Hamburg,

Germany. He had the novel idea of exhibiting animals in naturalistic settings instead of cages, and opened the first zoo of its type in 1907. He nods in appreciation as he sees the sign that says "Africa," and strolls toward me. It was he, almost 100 years ago, who began to display animals by geographic area instead of taxonomically where all cats or all primates would be together. Carl excitedly strides off to look at the Arctic Tundra and the Great Northwest areas.

Hot on his heels is William T. Hornaday, naturalist and taxidermist. With him is a group of finely clad gentlemen, swinging canes and puffing on cheroots. Hornaday created the living collection at the Smithsonian's Museum of Natural History in 1887, and in 1899 gave a critical shot in the arm to conservation efforts by becoming the director of a new zoo in New York. That zoo was heavily bankrolled by the men whom I now see jostling for a good viewing location at the giraffe exhibit. I melt back into the shadows to let them see the elegant giraffe pair drinking from the pool and flicking their ears against nighttime insects. The gang is impressive and includes Andrew Carnegie, John D. Rockefeller, Cornelius and William Vanderbilt, Levi P. Morton, William E. Dodge, and J. Pierpont Morgan.

I head for the viewing platform a few paces up, but find my visibility blocked by Teddy Roosevelt and other wealthy big-game hunters in the Boone and Crocket Club. They are clapping each other on the back and guffawing, pleased that their early efforts in protecting natural areas and the animals who lived there have lasted into this century. It is in the lifetime of our grandparents and their grandparents, that the American bison was almost wiped out and then brought back from near extinction to roam the plains.

Along the path I see imprints of animal footprints in the concrete. I've noticed them throughout the zoo and their effect is to make me "look both ways before crossing." These prints let us imagine that the game trails cross right under our feet and that the rustle in the bushes might be a small hippo that waddled past on its way to a watering hole, or the twitching tail of a small predatory cat looking for a rock hyrax or field mouse. Back in primitive times, this is how it was. Man walked around in a natural setting where many wild animals that shared the space were stronger, faster, and larger than he. Many were also potential predators and man most likely snuck and hid rather than strolled, because the name of the game was "eat or be eaten." I see the triangular hippo prints and get a sense that I am entering into *their* homes and as such, should behave like a polite and well-mannered guest, William Randolph Hearst, who built the world's largest private zoo in California, put signs along the road to his castle. They warned: "Always drive slowly — animals have the right-of-way." I think Gandhi would have approved of this thinking.

I sneak a glance at my watch and see that it is already a few minutes past closing time. Soon, the zoo security staff will appear from the shadows, pointing us to the exits and escorting us up the hill to the gates. Lights switch on in the barn and I hear the screech of metal as the rolling doors open to let the animals in for the night. The door with the "No Admittance" sign is guarded but for just a split second I imagine what it would be to slip in and wedge myself behind a supply cabinet and a barrel full of brooms and mops....

I feel the night breeze on my cheek as the door swings silently shut behind me, and I hunker down on my knees so I can peek past the storage area into the barn. Sounds of muffled hooves tell me that at least one of the giraffes is entering the stall, and I see the boots of two keepers on the other side of the barred gate. They are leading J.C. into a restraint chute, which is a huge metal grid that can hold her steady while they or a member of the veterinary staff examine her. She towers above me on impossibly long legs. I'm bowled over at how huge she is. A gentle giant, she bobs her head quietly and accepts a fresh chunk of carrot from the keeper with delicate lips. Her lashes flutter coquettishly and I am awed by her beauty.

The chute's doors close, trapping her in the metal cage with little room for movement. This is part of her daily training routine so she doesn't even flinch when a blood sample is taken from her shoulder. The keepers are logging her estrus cycle to monitor her fertility. They collect the data to understand more about the species, even though she is not currently scheduled to be bred.

If there was room with me in my imaginary hiding place, I might be joined by Dr. Betsy Dresser. She was the Director of Research at the Cincinnati Zoo years ago, and did ground-breaking research in successfully impregnating an eland with a bongo embryo which then had a successful birth. The great news was that an endangered species was successfully born from a host that was not endangered, giving us hope that we could use this novel approach and save some species before they became extinct. The intriguing part about Dr. D's story was that she had to transfer five embryos from San Diego to Cincinnati on a commercial airline but could not find a reliable incubator. The only consistently warm place to store and transport those five little ones was to tape the tubes to her armpit and have them travel there. She did so and history was made.

Although the routine blood tests and data collection that are done in Oregon and at other zoos might not be as exciting as her historical efforts, it marks a commitment on the part of zoos to do much-needed research on how these animals can be bred in captivity and hopefully saved as a species. A few years ago, 2,000 species were on the top of the endangered species list. Funding and interest existed to save 900, but the successful preservation of eggs, sperm and viable embryos was only available to nine. A sobering thought, indeed. Thankfully, we're slowly waking up from a long sleep and are beginning to shoulder responsibility for the animals that are left.

In my make-believe adventure, I slip out of the giraffe barn undetected. The pair is safely bedded down for the night with apples, alfalfa pellets, and sweet hay in their feeders and all around the zoo, other animals are being tucked in for the night. I start up the long sloping walk to the exit. I think back on the giraffes and what pleasant company they have been this afternoon. I reflect on all the past generations of people who defined their cultures by their actions and shaped the events of history that led us to today. I am deep in thought about what this means for me and my generation, when I realize I am not alone. To my right is Gandhi, who to my astonishment is licking the last of the soft swirl in a waffle cone. There is not much that can surprise me after the magic of tonight, but I him pictured with a cup of herbal tea instead.

"The first giraffe came to the U.S. in 1837," he says to me, as we pass the gift shop on the way out. A huge picture of a giraffe is on the window, bending down to look at us as we go through the turnstile. "Over a century and a half has now passed by. How will you care for the long-necks now?" he asks.

My mind races but the answer is not clear. I think of the hundreds of people we will need to commit their talents, their time and their hearts at this critical juncture. The best I can do is to think we can live our lives attentive to the question and perhaps one day, live into the answer as well.

Gandhi disappears into the night before I can respond. The next step is up to the people in this generation, I believe. The responsibility is in the hands of those who are already committed to the preservation of wild animals, and to those who are about to be. The moon has risen and is arcing across the sky. This day is almost over, but tomorrow a new day begins.

Wild Spaces for Wild Things

The blast of a high-powered shotgun thunders through the boulder-strewn woodlands of the Amur River valley on the Russia-China border. From high in a tree, a spotted bundle free-falls from a limb, shattered. The poachers will find him, pack him out of the woods, and sell his pelt and bones on the black market. Now, only 49 Amur leopards are left in the wild....

A mountain ridge away, his mate feels her stomach rumble. She is only a few weeks pregnant but already the fetuses demand more nourishment than she can easily provide. In less than three months the cubs will be born. She will have to teach them to survive the perils in the wild over the next few years, and keep them from new threats, such as people. The 30 square miles of range that she needs for hunting and shelter is rapidly dwindling, and it's harder to find the roe deer, wild boar, and hares that feed her and her young.

Roads and settlements are closing in, driving her food deeper into the rocky steppes and exposing her to the poachers that will come looking for her in the next month or two....

Enter, the Oregon Zoo.

> **Apartment Wanted:**
> **Older leopard couple looking for a quiet retirement home. Need a mix of furnishings for both climbing and resting. A warm dry place for relaxing very important.** [1]

Elmer and I peer into the exhibit, watching Frederick and Andrea dream leopard dreams as they snooze in a languid heap on the rock. Elmer is an elfin man of small stature and big heart, who has come through the zoo gates almost as many times as I have in the last few months. That's at least two dozen, last time I counted. Bedecked with a Nikon camera, assorted lenses, and a vest full of filters, he wears sturdy boots and rugged clothes, and sports leathery skin and a face traversed with lines of good humor. At the ripe old age of seventy-something, Elmer is entering his golden years. He avidly pursues photography in a way that he once only dreamed about, and spends countless hours hanging around the big cats.

---

[1] Exhibit sign, Oregon Zoo

Holding my small dog-eared notebook in my hand, I turn my face to the sun and give a lazy grin. It is mid-afternoon and hot, and a time for siestas or quiet conversations. I am half his age, and have only been at the zoo a short while. Still, I'm an astute observer, a decent writer, and a passionate thinker about the animals in this place. We are two of a kind, and look together in companionable silence, watching these magnificent specimens of *Panthera pardus orientulis* nap the afternoon away.

"I remember the old zoo," muses Elmer, crossing over to a bench and putting down his camera bag. "The place was small, very small, and was down the slope where the Japanese Garden is now."

"Yeah," I acknowledged, joining him on the seat and taking a long pull from my water bottle. "I just went there last week on a hike. What was the zoo like then?"

Elmer began exchanging his polarizing filter and macro lens. "I don't think it was a good set-up for the cats," he muttered. "Most of the cages were small. They didn't have waterfalls and foliage and such like that. There was a round set of cages and the public walked by each one. Each cage had an animal. I remember the hippo had a watering hole the size of a bathtub with a ramp that led down in it. There was barely room for him in there."

"Wow," I said, gazing at the luxurious natural exhibits that house many of the zoo animals today. "It's sure different now, isn't it?" Hippos are so ponderous that they need water to support their body weight. In the wild they spend a lot of their day submerged. Now, they gaze up at us from underwater in their 50,000-gallon exhibit pool. When the Northwest winters blow too cold for the hippos to be out, they loll around in tepid splendor in the 6,000-gallon private spas in the barn.

"Take this exhibit," Elmer said, nodding at the Amur leopard habitat across from us. He checked his camera and held it up to squint through the viewfinder. Lowering it, he began again. "This used to be like a cage. Bars on the sides, building in the back. Then the horticulture folks did some new-fangled research and figured out how to design a real nice space for the cats. It's the envy of other zoos, let me tell you!"

Warming to his topic, he stood up and motioned me to follow. "Look here." He pointed to the forested part of the 25 by 60-foot exhibit. "They got on the Internet and researched the Amur region of Russia where these cats are from. They brought in Amur maples, and local varieties of birch and aspen. Aspen is a good choice. Cats can claw and scratch them and they just shoot up suckers and grow some more." A nearby aspen had vicious three-inch gashes on its trunk, a testament to the power of the animals.

In contrast, Andrea gave an easy stretch and then rested her soft muzzle on Frederick's flank. Her eyes drifted closed, and she fell back to sleep. Weighing in at 78 pounds, she was dwarfed by Frederick's 128 pounds of lean muscle and looked more like his daughter than his littermate. They looked cuddly as can be — large house cats of the finest order. Both are 13 years old now, and could live another 10 years in captivity. They came here from another zoo just a few years ago and have adjusted nicely to the newly remodeled exhibit. So nicely, in fact, that it is a prototype that other zoos copy to encourage their captive cats to thrive and breed.

"Look down there," Elmer said, crouching and pointing to the understory. "There are ferns and shrubs so that it looks just like their homeland." Pointing to a trail circumnavigating the exhibit, he said, "And look at these paths. Betcha never seen anything like that!" I looked at the dirt path and saw nothing unusual. A few concrete pavers led the eye to the back of the space, smaller trails led through the trees, but there was nothing out of the ordinary.

"This is all thought out with a cat in mind," explained Elmer. "They figured where the cats would leap and climb and wander and made sure they could do it in this small space without getting hurt. The hort staff worked with the keeper to figure all this out, taking measurements and all. Leopards can jump 10 feet up and 20 feet across, so they figured that in. They carted in good dirt for the plants and rocks, and then made the paths with the clay you see on ball fields. Less weeds, for sure, and a hard-packed surface for the keepers to walk on. In winter, it gets pretty mucky here so the pavers help keep their boots dry. They gotta design it for the keepers as well as the cats, and this works for both of them."

All these years looking, asking questions and taking pictures had given Elmer an eye for detail and had made him a gold mine of information. "They made those climbing structures over there so that the place is 3-D. The cats can go up as well as all around and a small space can actually be much larger in terms of living space. You've got to think 'vertical,' when you look at a lot of the enclosures. That's what gives certain animals a sense of territory, space and freedom. Don't just count the square footage on the ground and think the cage is too small. In the winter, they like to hang out high up and catch some rays. It gives them a sense of security to see what's going on around them."

"But don't they want to hide out from people?" I asked. "These kids sure are noisy and the train depot is right here. There are so many people tapping on the glass, whistling, and making animal noises. Leopards are solitary by nature in the wild. How do they adjust?"

"I can't rightly say," said Elmer, rubbing his chin. "But I do know this for sure. Adjusting and adapting is the name of the game for endangered species, whether in the wild or at zoos. The keepers and the gardeners know the cats and their habits, and they do the right thing by the cats when they can."

"They've changed the exhibit to keep up with changes at the zoo. Take this road here." He jerked his chin to the walkway behind us, and went on. "The main entrance used to be further down in the parking lot, and everyone coming to the zoo walked by here. The cats here at that time got twitchy with all this commotion, so they put up a barrier of plants and trees to direct foot traffic. It kept the young kids from breaking through and running in and out, too. That's dangerous if a work truck is coming by. So they built up those trees and then ran a computer program to see how the sun would go and where shade would be. This is all scientific stuff. It's not just planting a tree or two and then taking off for lunch. It's animal management, public safety landscape architecture and exhibit design all mixed up in one!"

Movement brought our attention back as Frederick began to stir. He stood up, yawned, and padded off the rock to glide down a path thickly covered with vegetation. The leaves parted to allow his lithe body to slip through, and then fell back into place as if he was never there. I paused to wonder. In my lifetime, this disappearance could be the unhappy ending to the leopard story. In another decade, he and Andrea will probably die of old age. About 200 leopards are alive today in zoos such as ours, and like these, not all are breeding pairs. Of those who are, which will successfully breed? And of those, is there any chance that the young can be reintroduced into the wild and have the skills to survive? More importantly, will there be enough habitat to release them in, and will poaching still be a threat? Andrea seems unconcerned with my troubled speculations. She gets up, reaches her velvety paws out front and her rump in the air for a luxurious stretch, and pads over to the glass to peer out at the visitors.

"They're stimulated by the crowds," said Elmer, nodding. "They're curious about the noise of the train, the smells from the burger stand and the kids that visit from morning 'til night." He stopped for a moment, and then continued thoughtfully. "You know, they seem to like change. There's the seasons, for starters. Sunny 'n hot in the summer like now, and lotsa rain in the winter and spring. For a lot of the animals, this climate is different for them. Then there's the visitors. In the summer, you can get up to 10,000 in a day. In the winter? About 400, and most of them are old codgers like me with good rain gear against the wet."

"The keepers watch the animals for any signs of discontent. When the cats get to pacing or lose weight, or are more flighty or aggressive, the keepers look into it. They'll put scents out for the cats to smell, like wolf urine or ladies' perfume, spices or zebra dung. Anything to get those noses twitching. It's called "enrichment" and keeps them entertained. The keepers hide food in the cracks and crannies and up in the trees, so the cats have something to hunt for. Life can get too easy for Frederick and Andrea so the keepers figure out new ways to keep things interesting."

He moved past another new bunch of kids ooohhhing and ahhhhing at Andrea, pressing noses into the glass. At the next viewing area he hunkered down in a squat and pulled me down with him. "Look through the grasses there." He pointed with a gnarled finger, and I saw the view from ground level.

"Almost half the visitors to the zoo are under 3-feet tall. Kids, you know. Those kiddies have to be able to see or they are disappointed because they never got to see the leopards. In other exhibits without glass or bars, mom and dad lift them up to stand on the railings. Wild animals can move quicker 'n spit and would love to have one of the kid for lunch. No joshing. So the hort staff need to keep the grasses and shrubs hacked way down so everyone can safely see."

I peer around from this low vantage point and notice Frederick coming back from the depths of the exhibit. His golden eyes look steadily at me as he approaches with a purposeful walk. I draw back, a little frightened, and get quiet and still. There's something about being eye-to-eye with a carnivore that stirs an instinctual fear in my gut. I break eye contact so as not to instigate a challenge, but instead, enjoy the sleek slope of his shoulder and his long graceful tail. A small child comes beside me to look. She is three or four years old, cherubic and delightful. She jumps up in glee, and bumps the glass as she comes down. In a split second, Frederick pounces, moving more quickly than I thought possible. The child is oblivious, as is her mother, but I know what I just saw. To the leopard, this was fresh meat for the taking. I am glad for the glass between us. You just can't take the instinct of the hunt out of a wild animal.

I rise up and look around the exhibit some more. There is a kiosk in the shape of a house like those on street corners advertising places for rent.

> **Apartment for rent: Mid-sized zoo in Portland, OR, has space for two leopards. This newly remodeled exhibit contains many modern features, such as built-in heating pads, suspended walkways and running waterfall (fish included). Landscaping is gorgeous. Definitely a must-see. Hurry — space will go fast!**[2]

"How hard is it to maintain something like this?" I asked. Elmer thought for a moment. "It varies, of course, but as a rule of thumb they probably plant three times what they expect to survive. There's more than meets the eye. With cats, all the plants need to be washed to get rid of any trace of human scent. If

---

[2] Exhibit Sign, Oregon Zoo

they don't, the cats thrash it like catnip. Some of the exhibits don't work out and then it's back to the drawing board. They once designed a spectacular exhibit for the grizzlies with trees and shrubs neatly laid out. They let the two bears in and within 36 hours, it was grassland again. Everything was torn up. They put some maples in the elk area just a few weeks ago and they were okay for a few days. The next time the keepers went by, all the maples were lying on the ground, trampled. For the cats, you need to bring in the plants bit by bit, and they have to get used to it. It can take years of adding plant material to come up with an exhibit like this, but it's worth the effort."

He thought for another moment and then went on. "They also have to inspect any new plants to be sure they don't bring in unwanted insects or their eggs. Then they have to be sure they don't use pesticides that could harm the animals. It's a complicated thing, creating these spaces and maintaining them so that everything stays healthy, plants and animals alike."

"It's got to feel worth it, though, when you come up with something like this," I said, nodding at the replica of Amur woodland. The leopards were together now, gently nosing around in the stream and flicking their tails into the water. A small group of visitors was pressed against the glass, mouths agape, as they watched these beautiful animals from just a few feet away. "These animals really have a great life, all things considered!"

Elmer gave me a grin. "That's an interesting thing as well," he said with a chuckle. "Certainly, life is better for a zoo animal with these natural exhibits because they have more room and can interact with their environment. But what people think about an exhibit is not always how the animals see it. The keepers can study the animal and know what it needs — what sorts of places should be created for sleep and shelter, how much space to have between the climbing structures for them to jump and play, or how to keep the animals in the view of the public by putting heating elements in the tree crotches or food and water near the front of the exhibit. Sometimes people fool themselves and think that pretty flowers or a running stream makes for a good habitat, and that a plainer or more functional enclosure does not. If the place gets too overgrown, the cats can't protect their backs and can't see what's going on from a high perch. It can make them anxious and more jumpy and aggressive. People also think that the animals are better cared for when there is a pretty exhibit. It's not really true. If you're worried about cleaning out the stream or keeping trees from becoming a scratching post, you might not be spending as much time working directly with the animals or providing enrichment activities for them."

I had never looked at it that way. As a lover of plants, I am always drawn to what blooms or looks lush. I'm attracted to the sound of running water or the look of a still pond. I hadn't given a moment to think about its upkeep, or whether Frederick and Andrea shared my tastes in horticulture design! I look around some more, noticing the keeper door hidden near the back and the soft earth where leopard and human prints intermingle along the path. What a balance to maintain, in such a tiny microcosm. The keeper and the ones he or she cares for must both be considered to ensure the survival of this critically endangered species.

It's time for us to go now, so Elmer and I head back down the path. I have a better appreciation for all the zoo does to provide a habitat that these leopards can live in, and live well. The signs of feline contentment are before me — glossy fur, shiny eyes, normal body weight, and the absence of excessive pacing or other stereotypic behaviors. But what about in the woodlands of Russia, Korea and Manchuria? Will the leopardess successfully give birth and raise her cubs? Will the growing surge of human inhabitants make way for the simple maintenance or modest growth of a leopard population that is now critically endangered? I have thoughts swirling in my head but nothing definitive written in my notebook yet. What is my conclusion to the leopard story?

I move out of the way as a small herd of pre-schoolers come by. Pushing and shoving, they swirl around us like a small tidal wave and enter the viewing hut a few steps away. The kids shriek and holler, and plaster tiny sticky hands onto the transparent glass. Their eyes are aglow. Their parents crowd close behind them to look at the leopards. Andrea wanders up to the glass, rocks back on her haunches, and lifts two velvet paws to the glass. The size of her feet dwarfs their tiny fingers, but the number of kids seem to overwhelm her and she soon shrinks back. This is indeed a metaphor for her situation – she in her small corner of paradise versus the crowds that press in close.

Elmer and I back away to give the kids room, and watch child and cat eye each other with only a pane of glass between them. Each one is curious about the other. I have faith in the power of the pen as I write for and about these animals, but it is the power of that paw that will touch these children. They will remember the look in those golden eyes and will feel a loss when Andrea turns and disappears in the foliage. When these children grow with understanding and insight into adulthood, they will be the keepers, the zoo visitors and the writers, that care enough to see that she is protected and allowed to thrive.

I walk around a last sign on my way to the main path.

> No Vacancy:
> Space has been rented. New units in other zoos will be remodeled using techniques and practices perfected in this exhibit and critically endangered felines have priority. 23-year leopard lifespan leases approved but early move-out bonuses given for departures back to protected spaces in the wild.

E-Mails Home

January

Hi Dad,

 Great to hear from ya. Thanks for all the good wishes on my move to Portland. I'm moving furniture around, unpacking, and setting up my new home office. The computer works as you can tell by this e-mail. Yippee!

 You sound busy with all the end-of-year accounting stuff — sorting through your papers, getting rid of old files. It's the life of a CPA. I need to do that too. I can't believe all these jobs I've had in my life. I wonder, should I have spent 10 years refining my skills as a writer, instead of working as a secretary? How fast time flies! 10 years gone, whoosh!

 Next week I'll be looking for work. Probably some sort of office job to start with. Right now it's hard to sit still. I find myself going out to the garden every hour on the hour, to see what's going on. I'm also starting to write little reflections on the flora and fauna here in the Northwest.

February

Hi, Dad,

    Yes, I'll try not to get distracted from the job hunt. I know I need a professional job befitting my master's degree. I can't thank you enough for your help with my tuition and student loans!

    Jenn gave me a newspaper clipping on volunteer opportunities. It's nice to have a sister nearby who looks out for me. Did you know that the zoo in Portland has a horticulture program and needs volunteers? That could be fun. I might give them a call.

    I found some cool books when I was unpacking. Remember that one you gave me on my 13th birthday about the vet of the exotic animals? I still have it! I came across some animal stories I had written, too. They're not half bad!

March

Hi, Dad,

    Yes, I know that employers don't like it when you have breaks in your job history. I'm working hard at sending out resumes but it's only been 6 weeks so far. I just haven't found anything juicy yet. I hear that employers also don't like it when you skip around from career to career. If I can't list chronologically and I can't list categorically, what should I do? You've hired people for your accounting practice before. Any tips?

I have some free time since the job search is slow. I have a little shift at the zoo on Fridays to do the horticulture work that I mentioned in my last e-mail. The guys are really great — all of them seem to have degrees in horticulture by the way — and we're cutting down lots of bamboo for browse for the elephants, rhinos and musk ox.

March again
Hi, Dad,

Yes, you're right that a good way is to get an interview and then they'll see how great I am. I'm working on it. I also found my maroon power suit in the box, still wrapped in the dry cleaning plastic. It still fits. Whew! I hired a writing service to work on my resume like you suggested, and I guess they did a good job. It got real short though, once they took out all my volunteer work over the past few years. The way it's written, I can hardly believe it's me they're talking about. It's on a creamy linen bond which should sit well with the Fortune 500's out there. (smile)

I'm doing laundry now — lots of wet and muddy clothes. It was hard to think about interview suits today, for sure! We were slithering on our bellies in the snowy owl exhibit, hacking back sword ferns and pruning Douglas spirea and salal in an exhibit where there's not much room for humans. We had a great time visiting in the lunch room on our break. It's a relaxed camaraderie that I've always wanted at a workplace. I wrote an essay about it and was really charged up about the creative process. It's great feeling so much passion for writing and also being able to work outdoors.

April
Hi, Dad,

Hang in there! I know the last stretch of the tax season is always tough. Too bad you still haven't gotten outdoors for a hike since even your weekends are busy now. I know you love hitting the trails.

I'm on trails all right, but not moving very quickly. Most of my work as a horticulture volunteer is done on my knees. We're big into browse these days, chopping down truck-loads of bamboo for the hoof stock, pruning lots of new growth from trees and shrubs, worrying about toxic berries and sharp thorns on loads of mixed brush that's going to the primates, and digging out lots of irrigation pipe to make the annual repairs. I'm giddy. This is TOO MUCH FUN!

Not all my week is in the bushes, though. I'm doing more and more work with the animals and the public. Who has *time* to look for a job? Today is Packy's birthday. A nearby supermarket made a HUMUNGOUS cake and he sat on it. Packy is an elephant by the way. The largest one in North America. Thousands of people came to the party. I was busy from 7 a.m. until 10 p.m. decorating, handing out cake (3,500 pieces!), finding lost children, fixing the popcorn machine, and then loading bags and bags (and bags!) of trash into a truck and driving them to the dumpster. Whew! What a grand day! The press was there to take pictures and I'm still seeing spots from all the flashes.

May

Hi, Dad,

Yes, time sure flies! I haven't gotten the Sunday paper for a while but will be back at the job hunt soon, I promise. Yes, I know that persistence pays off. I've just been a little distracted lately.

Tuesdays at the zoo are now the highlight of my week, and we're planting trees, fixing irrigation systems, and checking out the model for the amazing new Salmon-Eagle exhibit that they're getting ready to build. I feel so accomplished. There's nothing like seeing progress every time you come to work! I'm signed up for the ZooGuide classes, which will let me do interpretive talks on the grounds. Remember that Toastmasters class you encouraged me to take so I could move up in the corporate ranks? It's really coming in handy here at the zoo. I've already been asked to do a presentation for a local business group about our wildlife education program.

June

Hi, Dad,

No, not really, I haven't gotten any calls for interviews just quite yet. I've been getting a lot of hang-ups on my machine lately. Maybe I need to be here to answer the phone in person. What do you think?

I changed the message on my answering machine and my friends just love it:

Roses are red, violets are blue,
If I'm not at my desk, I'm out at the zoo,
Talking to people, of bird, fish, and bear,
Of habitat loss I am making them aware,
Washing an elephant, feeding the seals,
Pruning the gardens, how good this all feels!
Please leave a message,
With name, date, and time,
But don't worry a bit,
If you can't make it rhyme.

It's kinda hard to be here at the house because the zoo attendance is picking up. 8,500 visitors today. Can you believe it? I'm helping to teach a class on birds-of-prey and got to hold a small Harris hawk on one of those cool leather gloves today. It was magical! I had to put in a lot of hours of training first, to be certified in bird handling. I also spent time preparing penguin food and got to pet Mo, the kitchen penguin. Remember when I was a kid and used to draw whales and penguins all the time? Now here's the real thing. They really *do* look like they are wearing tuxedos. Too cool!

I'm also taking up photography again. It would be great doing darkroom work again, or getting one of those new-fangled digital cameras and sending pics to all my friends. If I'm at the zoo before it opens for the public, I can get some great shots! I might try a little side business making greeting cards in my free time. I have a growing stack of fantastic ones and I feel very accomplished!

July
Hi, Dad,

Just got back from Office Depot where I stocked up on supplies. It's amazing how many reams of paper and ink jet cartridges you go through when you're writing a lot and printing out digital pictures. Oh, and composing drafts of cover letters. The job hunt is never far from my mind.

I'm writing more essays about volunteering here and am e-mailing them to all kinds of people at the zoo — my new ZooGuide friends, the volunteer coordinator, the marketing department, and even the director of the zoo! I got a magazine for writers and printed up some business cards that encourage people to get on my e-mail list. Did I tell you I set up a "virtual community" of 25 friends who get my newest essays at the end of every week?

The zoo concert series is now in full swing and I'm working security two nights a week, doing interpretive talks every weekday morning until noon, and helping with the interactive zoo classes all day

Saturday. I save Sunday just for me. It's great roaming around the zoo without my uniform, just enjoying the animals.

August

Dear Dad,

     What was that about wanting to see my resume? I'll see if I can find it. Maybe this weekend. But hey, my writing is going *really* well. I'm circulating essays to people outside the zoo now and am getting a very positive response. There's a job fair in town and I thought I'd go. I hear they have a table about self-publishing. I also got a cool zoo screen saver with polar bears on it. One is Conrad, our resident male. I probably have 10 snaps of him already in one of the big boxes where I store my photos. It's a growing collection, for sure!

     I won't be able to squeeze in a visit this summer as I usually do. I leave for San Diego next week to tour their zoo and the Wild Animal Park. I'm booked solid with interviews and meetings with their keepers and staff, so I scheduled an extra day just to lie on the beach and rest. There's a neat beach by Sea World. Maybe I'll just zip in to see what they're doing with the big sea mammals.

September
Dear Dad,

No time to write. I've just been hired as a seasonal staff person for the overnight program, and sleep over a lot at the zoo with the kids. Catch ya later!

October
Dear Dad,

Sure, I can come for a visit if you feel so strongly about it. I guess it's a good thing that I haven't found a full-time job yet, so I don't need to request vacation time!

At the zoo, the concerts are over and attendance dips pretty sharply after Labor Day because of cooler weather and the start of school. Yes, I know airfares are cheaper if it includes a Saturday but I don't want to miss the weekend crowd, small as it is. How about Tuesday through Thursday? If I return by noon, I can swing by Volunteer Headquarters on my way home to check the activity board for any new sign-ups. I'll be bringing my new laptop so I can keep up with my writing schedule.

November
Dear Dad,

It was great to visit. Thanks for changing everyone's plans and taking us all to the zoo down there. That was really great. I sure appreciated you taking me back the next day too. Two full days of zoo — I learned a lot! You got a little quiet at the end. Did your feet hurt?

I got back just in time to get my name on the sign-up sheets for a new series of interactive classes they're teaching. Parents and kids learn together, and they get to touch live animals. I was trained to handle most of the small animals (ferret, duck, chicken, iguana, snake, opossum) and just got my training from the insect zoo to handle the walking sticks and hissing cockroaches. What a thrill that was! Arthropods are fascinating, don't you think?

I've been down at the zoo all day, and at my desk all evening, catching up on various zoo projects. It's past midnight so I need to hit the sack. We're up early tomorrow morning to drive out to the condor preserve to get it ready for the birds. 16 are coming up from California in just two weeks. Can you believe it? Those birds have a 9-1/2 foot wingspan!

December

Hi, Dad,

I just went through my file cabinets to make room for zoo stuff. There were a bunch of old transcripts, letters of reference and old job applications. It was great to throw them all out. Gad, it seems like so long ago when I first moved here and started looking for work, but it's only been a year. What a ride it's been!

Life here is grand. I'm skipping out on two holiday parties, and instead am hanging out at the elephant barn watching them train the girls. It takes your breath away. I can't figure out why it's so amazing to see these gargantuan animals, comical and cute, dangerous as heck, trotting around the yard with grins, putting wrinkled butts carefully down on drums and raising their columnar legs into the air in response to keeper commands. It's simply wonderful! I'm sitting there grinning, and understanding what makes someone want to be a keeper when he or she grows up. Where else can you be in the presence of so much mystery and wonder, with the unexpected always around the next corner? We spent four hours bolting together strips of fire hose to make a hay net for the elephants this afternoon. I guess this is why I didn't get a paid job as an office manager or something, as I always threatened I'd do.

You said someone was going to call me about a part-time bookkeeping position today? I must have missed the call. Whoops.

January
Hi, Dad,

Happy New Year to you! I'm glad you've renewed your accounting license and look forward to another year of doing taxes and financial management. Good for you. I was impressed by your list of last year's accomplishments and your itemized goals for the coming year.

I, on the other hand, have a much stranger list. In the last year I was licked by a rhino, touched the wiry hairs of an elephant, and petted a penguin. I've taught hundreds of zoo visitors about crocodiles, giraffes, and Steller sea lions. I've been sneezed at, trampled by, and clambered on by too many children to mention. I made friends with several dozen volunteers, found camaraderie with the staff and keepers, understand a teensy bit more about what goes on behind the eyes of the bears and tigers and snakes, and think one of the orangutans has a crush on me. I've plodded through the autumn rain, sweated through the summer sun, and tiptoed through the crystalline wonder of a freak winter snowstorm that blanketed the zoo in all its finery. I've hauled sand to furnish condor nests, helped capture a loose guinea fowl, and cut browse for hippos and grizzlies to munch on and play in. I've made a speech, gotten awards, saw my ideas solidify into things that make the zoo a better place, and still feel bubbly and giddy every time I enter those front gates.

I still don't have an office job, but realize I don't want one. I was looking for purpose and meaning, excitement and adventure, and I found it here at the Oregon Zoo.

Snowy Owls and the Good Life

A downy brown-and-white feather sits on my palm, ruffled gently by the evening breeze as the summer day cools into night. Just yesterday it was part of a species of bird that is usually seen only in the chilly vast expanse of the Arctic Tundra. What a gift to be nose-to-beak with this creature, as he hooted his indignation at my trespass into his territory.

The portion of the zoo labeled Arctic Tundra is a mysterious place. Strollers, wheelchairs and the patter of many feet travel down a gentle ramp and enter through the heavy doors. Darkness envelops you. When your eyes adjust to the dim lighting you thread your way past lighted displays, a video documentary of Arctic life, and what looks like holograms of a pair of caribou that repeat themselves endlessly into the distance with the help of artfully placed mirrors. Northern lights shimmer overhead, and the soft carpet muffles footsteps as you silently enter this magical wonderland. The winding hall pulls you along and pushes you outdoors to the animal exhibits. You can see a grizzly lolling in a pond and flexing his 3-inch long claws, catching apples thrown to him by his keeper. Next is a trio of shaggy musk oxen lumbering up the grassy slopes of their enclosure. They look placid even with their magnificent horns, but the trained eye sees the battered plastic barrels and the logs scraped bare and knows these are not docile creatures! Their recreational activities include brutal shows of strength and aggression, yet cold weather can bring them shoulder-to-shoulder nuzzling one another's neck in gentle companionship. Last is a sampling of birds characteristic of the Arctic. These ducks and owls sleep, feed, breed and regularly patrol their naturalistic habitats searching for food and watching for predators which never come.

I am privileged to be a horticulture volunteer and have weekly assignments as part of a team of gardeners. One task is to re-balance the flora with the fauna of each exhibit. It seems that the gardeners have done too good a job over the years with luxurious and striking foliage at every turn. Now, the overgrowth is keeping people from viewing what they have paid to see! We are scheduled to work on the snowy owl exhibit this morning, but the keeper who holds the keys and shoulders the responsibility for their care is detained. We use this time to our advantage and see what we can do for the ducks in the enclosure next door.

Three humans and three ducks are not a good mix. We enter with large yellow debris cans, pole pruners, and an assortment of rakes and loppers that throw the ducks into an explosion of alarm. It is all I can do to balance on the rim of the pond and not fall in headfirst when the mottled brown female sails out from undercover with strong flaps of her wings. The overhead netting stops her just when she is getting some speed and loft. She ricochets off and comes arcing back like a misguided boomerang. We drop to our knees and lower our tools so as not to skewer the frantic bird. She catapults back to safety with an ungraceful splash and hurried paddle.

We begin pruning and pulling weeds. The ducks continue to intermittently burst out of hiding with quacks and wing flaps to the safety of the far pond. There is no cover there yet they are creatures of habit. They catch their breaths and launch back to return to their habitual nesting site, right under our heavy boots, falling boughs, and dangerous equipment! My heart goes out to them as I realize they don't understand the confines of this man-made home, and can't puzzle out where safety really is.

In a manmade world, what is the bigger force in *my* duck-like existence that clucks in sympathy as I, too, rush back to safety when I'm really returning to what is no longer safe? I've watched myself yearn to return to traditional work, when free-lance writing or consulting seemed like too much work for too little pay. I had almost convinced myself I wanted to return to a cubicle and surround myself with co-workers, to be spared the long hours and relative isolation of my current situation. But I am older now, and clearer about what my contributions are in the world.

Ultimately there is no safety in going back to a regular paycheck or an 8-to-5 routine. Like the waterfowl, I'd do best to look for new places to paddle and to seek nutritious food that feeds both my belly and my soul.

We haul barrel after barrel of weeds and tree trimmings down a steep stairwell of cement steps with closed-in walls. I can only imagine that this is what the old zoos were like. There's the heavy-duty chain link fencing, some machinery that looks like a generator or compressor, brooms and buckets, and yards and yards of dull-gray concrete. The "realness" of this behind-the-scenes view contrasts with the naturalistic exhibit that the visitors see — artfully constructed boulders, carefully chosen plants, and perches and shelters designed and built to the exacting specifications of what each species needs and prefers. The three bird displays are close together in a pie-wedge arrangement, and as I take the barrels down, I am at eye level with the animals next door. Two snowy owls live here who need to be relocated while we work in their home.

The keeper finally arrives and he crouches amidst the waist-high grasses, enticing his "prey." Snowy owls are very territorial. One has been aggressively rushing at me from the other side of the fence each time I pass by. The keeper knows this, and beats his gloved hand against a rock to bring out that fighting urge. After two or three aborted attempts, the owl makes a run at him with a screech and a vicious grasp of outstretched talons. The keeper is able to throw another gloved hand over the bird's back and wings, keeping away from the scimitar-sharp beak which can swivel more than 180-degrees to relieve him of a finger or two. His grip is firm yet somehow tender, as he bundles the bird off to safety.

The second owl is more docile and is caught without a hitch. Perhaps this owl is accustomed to the routine and has the adaptability to rise above the terror of capture by a potential predator and rest calmly in those capable hands. I sense the energy of the keeper and he is a kind man. He works with the natural instincts of the birds and does what is necessary to keep a wild animal captive in the best way possible. He takes his gentleness across the barrier between two species and enters the world of the wild ones with a loving touch.

I don't know his story but the keeper may have been there when the first owl pecked his sleepy way out of a warm speckled egg. He may have brought in a sleeping bag for night feedings if the bird needed to be hand-reared. He may have read books and e-mailed keepers at other zoos. I'm sure there were hurried conferences with other keepers, conservation and veterinary staff at the zoo, on how best to deal with each bruised wing, chipped beak, or overgrown talon. There is an intricate history and reservoir of knowledge behind every decision he makes that I can only imagine.

We enter the vacated exhibit with a gas-powered weed whacker. For the next half hour the roar of the equipment drowns out any attempts at conversation. We prune the larger shrubs and trees, handing piles of limbs and branches from one to another until we can work them down the set of steep concrete stairs and into our barrels. It is a small exhibit and we do most of our work crouched over. It is humid and hot and the work is strenuous.

I find myself under a fern, breathing the dampness and snipping last winter's dark brown fronds. Earthworms wriggle up in the moist earth and a myriad of unidentified crawly things run for cover. Mark, the staff gardener, is trimming a lilac with an artful efficiency brought on by 27 years in this job. He knows his plants, he knows the Arctic Tundra, and he knows how to bring about an aesthetic balance between flora and fauna and between viewer and captive animal. Rob, a hort volunteer like myself, is everywhere, handing us our sweating water bottles, carrying out debris, pulling four foot high weeds from within the thickets, and trimming small trees that are already poking their crowns through the netting that keeps the birds from soaring off in search of their native homeland.

With our noses to the ground, we all spot curious details of the owls' lives in captivity. I find a metal washer, part of a pink baby pacifier, a paper candy wrapper and a piece of tin foil. Any of these swallowed by the owls could mean death and this type of careless litter is a problem in all zoos. Rob shows me a desiccated mouse lodged in the crook of a dwarf conifer. Hidden food acts as "enrichment" for the birds, and these treats hidden in the exhibit let the owls have a sense of foraging for their meals as they would in the wild.

Mark checks sprinkler heads and the health of the pond and artificial stream that feeds it. He mentions that the zoo can spend over $60,000 per month on its water bill. I begin to understand the extent of the zoo budget and what is needed to cover simple maintenance of the grounds. There are hundreds more details that go into the care and keeping of these animals, yet the public pauses for less than a minute at an exhibit before moving on. Most will never give a passing thought to the volunteers, gardeners, keepers, conservationists, research personnel, support staff and administration that add up to hundreds of people who live and breathe this complex world, working around the clock to keep it healthy and thriving.

Children and adults pass the exhibit as we work, and we overhear some thought-provoking comments. A young girl announces to her family in an outraged voice that we are "destroying their habitat!" I do not take offense, but rather am impressed that at such a young age, she understands the concept of habitat and is bothered enough by this perceived trespass to speak out. I'm glad that she thinks beyond her designer shorts and the waffle cone in her hand, and extends her heart to the creatures that are here for her to see and learn from. I don't correct her by explaining that we're just managing the cover so that birds and people can see one another. I want her to keep her outrage, continue to look and learn, and one day take an informed stance to the policymakers who will continue to represent a strong environmental conscience and support habitat preservation.

What do her folks think of this? Her dad wears a tee shirt from a recent Audubon fundraiser and mom wears hiking boots that have seen many a mile. I hope they take the time, on days other than this zoo outing with the kids, to saunter down forest trails and watch the sunset and the moonrise with the whole family in tow. Perhaps they are zoo members or even ZooParents who have adopted an animal somewhere in the zoo, creating a personal link to this magical place and making a financial statement in how they want to support the work that is being done here.

They are pushing 40 and are young, relatively speaking. Will they refuse to be overwhelmed by the threat of terrorist attacks, pollution in the Columbia River, smog alerts in our Willamette Valley, and genetically modified tomatoes, so that they continue to address these concerns and do their small yet essential part? Do they do those daily things like fill their recycling bins, eat lower on the food chain, drive a gas-efficient or hybrid car, and infuse their children with care and consideration for the plants and animals they live amidst? I turn back to the crispy brown sword fern frond, give it a thoughtful snip with my pruners, and hope it is so.

We work in an area that is no larger than a bedroom. The over story of dwarf trees closes in the space, and the netting above puts a cap on an environment which is miniscule if one compares it with the range of a wild bird out in the tundra. Giggles, shrieks, and normal conversations all funnel past concrete walls into the plants, grasses, rocks, and water, and seem to be amplified. I take it all in and then put myself in the place of an Arctic duck or a snowy owl. With hearing many times more acute than ours, a body size just a fraction of ours, and a daily dependence on receiving food from us, how can these animals stand the stress of a life in captivity?

If I were a bird, I would be in a constant state of pacing, feather fluffing and beak clacking, just to relieve the nervous tension and throw off some of this energy that intrudes into my space. I ask Rob about this since he is a retired forest ranger. He replies that the owls looked content but he didn't think they would breed. "What sort of life is that," I ponder, "without the normal cycles of mating, raising young, migrating, and having the freedom to respond to the wide open spaces of the tundra, soar among the northern lights, or experience that aching silence of a frosty winter day in that open land?" I learn later that the female occasionally *does* lay eggs, so I am confronted again by how little I really know or understand.

Many zoo animals can live twice as long as their wild cousins. They enjoy a secure source of food, shelter and veterinary care, which is unheard of in nature. Animals might come to our zoo from other facilities to be part of a breeding program, and care is taken to create the best possible conditions for success. For other animals, the reality is that their fate would have been certain death in the wild. Some may have arrived here broken and thin, diseased and dirty, rescued from roadsides and run-ins with cars or hunters. Others come from animal shows, research labs, circuses, and private collectors or zoos ill-equipped to care for them. Only a tiny minority of the animals were collected as healthy specimens from the wild many years ago — a practice that is no longer common with North American zoos today.

I can roam through the zoo with a clear conscience, knowing that an animal may be arthritic or diabetic, old or blind, unable to breed or unable to chew its food unless it is pureed. I am getting to know some of the keepers and see their gentle hands and warm hearts. I hear stories of the vets and vet techs and the lengths they go to provide compassionate and humble care for the animals that are on their watch. Yes, the snowy owl exhibit is a little small and a little loud, but there are mice in the crooks of the branches, a caring keeper ten yards away, and hundreds of children's eyes that light up as they learn about these birds that look back at them with golden eyes.

Our debris barrels are full to bursting and we are losing steam. It's hard physical work and we've been at it for a couple of hours. We break for lunch and head back to the shop where we strip off our wet jackets and shake off leaf and dirt debris. Over sandwiches and fruit, we wonder out loud how the owls will like our work. It is clear that we work on their behalf and, although we cannot get into their minds, we do our best to create places that they'd enjoy for sunning, sleeping, perching and feeding.

There is time to return to the exhibit to see how the birds are adjusting to their re-landscaped digs. We follow the surge of the crowd to see the display from the visitors' side. The ducks swim unperturbed. They accept the fact that their cover is now half as dense and their pond is still littered with some leaves and twigs. They have no choice. Neither do we. If I could be a genie, I'd grant them a large and wild place where the cycles of the seasons would prune and plant for them. I'd bring in another hundred of their friends, to give them a wider choice of mates and more animals to socialize with. I'd put humans out of sight and out of scent so that the animals were undisturbed. But they are here for us to experience and this is a dilemma for the zoo — how do you balance the needs of the animals with those of the viewer?

In the next area the dominant snowy owl comes running through the now-short grass, looking almost comical as if he's wearing white trousers and a coat with tails. He flaps his wings and hoots at us, but not with much fervor. Perhaps he is weary from the excitement of the morning and just hopes for some quiet repose. The display looks good though, and we are pleased. There are still places for frozen mice to be hidden and for him to find them as he forages. There are snags for perches, clean water to drink, and a companion who peers out from under the lilac bush. His keeper respects his wildness and tends to his needs with care and consideration. For most of the thousands of families that could come to the zoo each day at the height of the summer, this will be their only look at the snowy owl outside the pages of a National Geographic magazine or away from the action on a PBS documentary on tundra birds. Perhaps it is not so unconscionable to display a pair of these noble birds for that end.

I leave the zoo tired from crouching and climbing, pruning and weeding. My head is full of compassion for the animals, understanding of their needs, and realization of the fine line that gardeners, keepers, and other zoo staff tread in bringing these animals to us. The evening breeze is picking up as the sun sinks down for the night.

I go out to my garden for a last breath of the summer evening. I savor my freedom to travel far if I choose, forage for my own food in my vegetable plot or grocery store, and choose my own mate and habitat when I find what is to my liking. Is it in the restrictions of another that we find our own freedom? Perhaps it is in the wildness of that captive animal that we find perspective for our own lives and can recommit to being a steward for theirs.

Taxonomy or Tenderness?

There's a junior taxonomer in me fighting to get out. Give me a tidbit of nomenclature and I've been known to get a pompous tilt to my head, puff my chest out a bit, and rattle off a Latin genus and species name to the open-mouthed wonderment of all. Admit it — can't you think of a time when you'd rather refer to our tree kangaroo as *Dendrolagus matschiei* than as its humble stable name of Blaze? Doesn't *Hylobates syndactylus* sound more impressive than Leslie, the name of one of our siamang monkeys? Maybe it's how it rolls off the tongue. Or maybe it's the mystery of an ancient language that catalogs our animals according to a lineage that started before our ancestral genealogical charts begin. But when I think about this a little deeper, I don't like it. Fancy words create distance between us and the beating hearts that pump inside the animals of the zoo. I want to cuddle with something named "Delilah" or "Coco," rather than *Pan troglodytes* (that's a chimp, by the way).

Upon graduating from training, Volunteer ZooGuides are handed a small notebook that contains information on every zoo animal. The cards list taxonomic names as well as common names (penguin, musk ox) and stable name (Garnet, Suzie) which are what keepers sing out when it's feeding time, training time or they just want to say hello. The bigger the animal, the more likely it is that we've given it a name. Mammals are the most commonly named. Then come the education animals that go to schools, and the birds of prey that are trained for shows and demonstrations. When you get down to non-show birds, reptiles, rodents and fish, there's an absence of labels we can use to interact with them.

Practicality rears its ugly head. After all, why call an iguana or a fruit bat by name if it's not likely to respond? Why name a whole colony of naked mole rats when it's hard to tell one from the other? Our notebook says of mole rats, that "the numbers in the collection change frequently." We'd be hard-pressed to find names all starting with "A" for the first batch of eight, then "B" for the next litter, and so on. The short-lived creatures like butterflies may also go from birth to death without a name for us to put in the logbook or file with the registrar. After all, their life spans are often just 7-10 days! Still, I have a big heart and a soft spot, and think we ought to make an investment in the small, short-lived and less popular species. Hence my fascination with the Insect Zoo.

I still remember the day when conversations in passing and then in excited group huddles spread the word that a birth had occurred. Several in fact. *Exatasoma tiaratum* had oodles of babies! The horticulture team fanned the embers of the announcement into a roaring fire, gassed up the trucks, and drove them out to sites far and near to collect the choicest blackberry vines to feed the hungry youngsters. Staff were admonished when cuttings were too thick: *"They need to be the tender new shoots, smaller in diameter than your little finger."* Buckets were rinsed out for the delicate young snippings the crew collected, and we all tromped over to the birthing room to offer up our booty.

Exatasoma tiaratum is the Australian walking stick, a curious insect that settles her 4" length quite comfortably in your warm palm. She's often tan with darker brown accents, and looks like a handful of dried leaves strung together on a twig. Adults grow darker with time, like detritus on a forest floor melting into mulch. The nymphs belong to another color palette altogether and are black with cute red heads!

I pressed my nose to the glass and watched the new family demolish a bouquet of blackberries arranged in a glass vase. Males are slim with wings for flight. Females are thicker and earthbound, turgid with the bounty of unlaid eggs. They'll lay 100-200 over several months, one at a time, and we were seeing the first hatchlings that had come to life. The leaves were slowly but steadily torn off and consumed by the busy youngsters. Gardeners had their marching orders to collect new fodder for the following day.

The Insect Zoo is an interesting phenomenon. Housed in a converted concessions stand and standing across from the pump room of the sea lion exhibit, it could easily be overlooked. Throughout the winter months, the only footprints going in and out are those of the keeper. Madagascar hissing cockroaches molt and their discarded carapaces litter the terrariums like squadrons of dead soldiers after an unfortunate battle. The tarantula and scorpion spend more of their hours basking by the heat lamp or snuggled under a warm rock because of shorter days and precious little sunlight during this rainy, misty time. Short-lived insects may die off. Their empty cages await a new order that will be shipped by express mail in carefully designed packages, bringing new lodgers to awe and delight us. By and large, insects have no christening ceremony and no name to welcome them into the world when they arrive at the zoo.

ZooTeens run the Insect Zoo in the prime time between Memorial Day and Labor Day. Zoo attendance zooms upward as school gets out, vacationers flood the gates and warm sunny days bring us all out to play. The teens are trained to handle the fragile walking sticks that step cautiously to the edge of their palms and peer out at the kids gathered to see. They gently sway to and fro, mimicking the effect of a breeze rustling the leaves of a branch on which they rest. The female can extrude an egg on the top of her tail that curls over her back. She can then fling it through the air to give her youngster a new start on a bush far away. With knowledge comes a connection, and with connection comes a sense of caring. Why not name her Genevieve or Heloise and celebrate the wonderment of her existence, as she shivers in an imaginary wind and seeks to catapult her progeny to multiply in the world?

ZooTeens also hold the weight of the world in their hands when they hold a Brazilian cockroach for the public to see. Without cockroaches to eat the decomposing vegetation, animal remains and bat guano in the forests of Brazil, we'd end up with a stinky heap of dead stuff. Without bees, moths and other insects to pollinate the fruits and vegetables that we magically see on the grocery store shelves each day, agriculture as we know it would end. Think of the food chain where you need 1000 plants to feed 100 mice which in turn feed ten bald eagles. We cannot forget the little insect guys at the beginning, when we're focusing on the mega carnivores at the end! The six-legged ones deserve names. They've earned them.

I love the creeping, crawling denizens of the Insect Zoo. How can you *not* have a regal name for the Emperor scorpion, *Pandinus emperator*? King Tut, Emperor Zhou, or His Regalness Pandinus, all have a nice ring to them. The Madagascar hissing cockroaches draw the attention of every kid within a 50-foot radius so why not name them Arpicuno, Magby or Gyarados after Pokemon characters? Sure, there are a lot of baby Australian walking sticks, but why not name the young 'uns Chip, Splinter and Toothpick, and really get to know them?

Let's bypass the Latin genus and species, on our way to a personal connection of recognizing each poison dart frog in the terrarium or lorikeet in the aviary. I propose that we name all the animals in the zoo, Insect Zoo tenants included. Let's honor them all with names, log them in the books and retire them like a quarterback's jersey number when the insect passes away. Let's all stop by and stroke the underbelly of the Giant African millipede and feel the feathery antennae brush against our fingers, and learn if her name is Millie, Eleanor or Gertrude. We hold her gently, care about her young, and wish her a happy life. When we distinguish her from the other two in the tank and begin to know her preferences and habits, we make that close connection that moves from taxonomy to tenderness.

Eagle Canyon

"And the end of all our exploring will be to arrive where we started and know the place for the first time."
— *T.S. Eliot*

I go to the zoo to come home. There is an irresistible draw for me to contribute, see the beauty, or just breathe in the air and breathe out my awe. I can inhale something indefinable and that act of breathing it in gives me life. I grin at the cartoon-like silhouette of the meerkats as they stand like sentinels by their burrows. I'm dazzled by the peacock that parades by the staff entrance and ruffles his turquoise and gold feathers like a flamenco dancer. I'm perplexed by the impossible horns of our rhino that should by all rights make him cross-eyed. My appearance is so different from them, yet somehow they are "understandable kin." I feel among family here.

I called my real kin last week. I had a rigorous volunteer day with the horticulture crew, working on a new zoo exhibit called Eagle Canyon. Mom answered my phone call brightly, cheerful after a late-afternoon nap. I was subdued, exhausted if you care to know. 10:00 a.m. to 2:00 p.m. was the shining gem in the busyness of my day and I'd spent that precious time in boots, raingear and a hardhat, sliding down muddy trails preparing a new home for a pair of bald eagles. I was bone-tired, my back was one big ache, and even my finger joints and tendons hurt from hauling pairs of five-gallon buckets filled to the brim with wet sand and clay. I whined on the phone to my mom about the rain and the mud, the strain of lowering 300-pound trees down a chute to the canyon below, the meager lunch I had packed, and the protests of my body whose muscles were tied up in a perpetual question mark of overexertion. The mind and heart were willing. The body asked: "*Who, me?*"

Like a lioness protecting her cub, she countered with fierceness: "When it's cold or raining you stay home. Just say you have the sniffles." Outraged, I wailed, "But it's *always* cold and raining in Oregon. And I'm not sick. I *want* to be there!" There was a silence over the telephone as we both collected our thoughts. She sifted through possibilities to save me from injury or terminal fatigue. After some pleasant chit-chat about the weather and when we'd get together next, I hung up.

I picked at the earth under my fingernails, slid into a deeper slouch in my chair, and as I relived recent memories in the Canyon, a smile came to my lips. My body stayed still, collapsed into the chair, but my mind raced back to the planting site. I remember standing on a slope below the viewing area where our volunteer crew was circled around an existing tree. We had hauled in a dozen trees to re-vegetate the floor of the new bald eagle exhibit, and were now digging shallow holes to position them. Next week, soil would be blown in with a hose from a truck parked high up in the parking area, creating an instant landscape. As we took turns with the shovels, I spaded a heavy clod of clay and levered it into a waiting bucket. *"Isn't it amazing,"* I mused, to no one in particular, *"that this might be the first time a shovel has ever touched this piece of soil in the history of the planet?"* We all had to rock back, lean on our shovels, and think about it for a minute.

Later at lunch, I munched my apple and chewed on the irony of our work. My rearrangement of this virgin soil is part of a multi-million dollar effort of the Oregon Zoo to house and protect the bald eagle, a species that was almost annihilated with DDT just a few decades ago. As our population burgeons every upward, farmers are pressed to grow more food in smaller spaces and keep it pest free. Pricey mistakes are made in our learning process. We once sprayed crops with DDT to protect against insects. Fish ingested the tainted insects and the poisons were concentrated. Bald eagles then ate the fish and consumed what were now highly toxic doses of DDT. The birds laid eggs that had thin shells and generations of eagle chicks never developed past the yoke stage before being crushed under the weight of their bewildered parents. Once we stopped using DDT and the poison ran its course through all the levels of the food chain, bald eagles could again incubate and raise healthy chicks. Thankfully their numbers started to increase. Whew! That was a costly mistake.

They say we learn from our mistakes and as an individual, I make my share of them. Just the other day I cashed in some frequent flyer miles in a promotion that promised free magazine subscriptions. I checked the boxes on several of them, dreaming up a justification for each one. *Organic Style* would let me know what's up with tofu and home improvement with green materials. *National Geographic* would regale me with news and pictures from the other side of my planet. *Kiplinger's* would give me financial tips so I could continue to write and live off the spurts of interest and dividends that found their monthly way to my checking account by electronic transfer. *Field and Stream* would show me what men think and why hunting is a good thing, so maybe I could catch a man and again enjoy the bliss of married life. *Health Magazine* would remind me to walk daily, meditate nightly, and see a chiropractor monthly.

When four of the magazines arrived in one day causing an alarming tilt to my mailbox, I stopped right in the driveway to flip through the pages. What I saw and read were instructions on what to eat, how to sleep, what to wear, and how to build my financial wealth. Seeing pencil-slim models with false smiles and bare feet squeezed in high-heeled shoes, made my toes curl in sympathy in the comfort of my well-worn sneakers. Defining happiness in terms of wealth and net worth seemed cliché and unexamined. I called the 800 number the very next day to cancel all my subscriptions and felt like I'd purged my mind of something as invasive as the English Ivy we'd spent part of the day clearing from Eagle Canyon.

I can probably learn more about what is real and right about the world by spending time each week in my volunteer horticulture shift at the zoo. I can explore questions like: *"Where is my place in the scheme of things on this planet?" "What daily activities can help me stay strong and limber, balanced and energized?" "In whose company can I feed my spirit, my soul and my muse?"* And most importantly, as far as the zoo is concerned, *"What can be done to rebalance the environment, so that plants and animals can thrive in a healthy co-existence with man?"* I trust the wisdom of hands-on experiences far more than articles in glossy magazines. A shovel full of virgin soil in my hands makes me think, and extracts a sheen of sweat and some hours of my time before giving me a few answers.

I have a fascination with the process of creating Eagle Canyon. It is a totally new exhibit for the zoo, yet its theme is the Northwest in which we live. It's a concentrated microcosm of what we'd see if we took the time to wander through our *own* woods and the surrounding mountainsides. At the time of this writing, the bones are in — a muddy trail that hairpins down to a natural creek, a covered bridge and viewing platform, a tunnel housing tanks and terrariums, and a viewing bubble so we can circle around with the salmon in their underwater world.

On any given day it's a beehive of activity. Wiry men women winch bundled trees up steep inclines, artisans sit on scaffolding shaping rebar and chicken wire into boulders and waterfalls, and an ant-like stream of industrious workers go up to the light or drop down into the dimness of the canyon with concrete saws, pond liners, urgent messages and forgotten lunch bags. We work hard with a dual agenda. Visitors come to the zoo to be entertained but we are committed to educating them. We lure them into a small section of woods that looks like their own northwest forest, and pique their curiosity. They can peer into the depths of the eagles' nest or tip a cup of water on a mountain model and see how runoff forms watersheds. In the guise of fun we captivate them with a place where they learn, love and remember.

I feel honored to be part of this. There is much time spent and much sweat shed as we cut a flight corridor for our eagles through the thickly intertwined tree branches. We hike up to vantage spots, triangulating with squinted eyes to be sure the birds can fly from the first to the second to the third artificial snag and perch comfortably. A branch here, a limb there, shouts and grunts, and soon we shape the existing thicket so that two eagles can have a small but safe life here. Next week we'll lay a pond liner for the marsh exhibit, creating something natural that might have existed here before we put our messy footprint upon the land.

The week after? We might plant the understory of ferns and salal for the trees we just heeled in. We'll sprinkle bark, bits of branches, dead fern fronds and brown pine needles to create "duff" — the layer of naturally occurring decayed matter on the forest floor. We'll carefully pull up carpets of moss from deeper in the woods, cut them to size, and lay them on artificial boulders to replicate the damp green beauty of a shady sylvan hillside. We'll bring the native plants back, but most will be ordered from nurseries and greenhouses. It will take horticulturists with degrees and volunteers with careful coaching to recreate a natural scene, and it will be attended to with painstaking detail. These are the dues we pay — our reparation.

The next time I feel the call, I will wedge a crack into my busy schedule so my muse can slip in. Down I'll go, to Eagle Canyon. I'll press my cheek against the cool glass and watch a mighty Kokanee salmon glide by, her olive green eye swiveling as she meets my blue one and we connect as one species to another. I'll sit on a bench in a fern grotto and lean back to look high up on a snag. A bald eagle will be there. She'll fluff her feathers and preen, as the afternoon breeze winds down the canyon and caresses her mighty wings. I'll make notes in my well-worn notebook about what I see and hear and feel about where my life is leading me. Do fish and birds wonder? Do they also pause and consider their lives? For me, faith often floods in to fill the spaces left by questions of how my life will go. Do those with fins and feathers also have a "knowing" that reassures them of yet another tomorrow?

I have time to explore as our horticulture team takes its lunch breaks or I am sent on frequent errands to fetch and carry. The newly fashioned waterfall is often my chosen lunch spot. I begin to see and understand how we mimic the real thing with artful placement of rock and foliage. I can anticipate where the spring's moss will grow, the summer morning's dew will condense, and the dried leaves of autumn will gather. As the sun slants in the canyon and walks its gleaming fingers across its length, I can understand how dawn will first appear to wake the bald eagles and where warm spots will migrate across the stones and snags throughout the day. I might be tempted to sip from the natural creek or nap on a sun-drenched ledge. I will see my desires and the eagles' narrow into one — space, sun, beauty — and will see the terrain from their eyes. Perhaps months down the road when our work on the exhibit is done, I will spend time not working but just being. I will rest in the splendor of the stream, the rocks, and the trees.

There is an energy in this place that filters back to the animals. At this zoo our actions show our caring. Dozens of hands have positioned these rocks, watchful eyes have seen that plants take root and flourish. Countless men and women have lain awake at night fretting over details and deadlines. Throughout the verdant spring, administrators and corporate sponsors have filed down these uneven paths in wing-tipped shoes and plastic mud-splattered hard hats, watching a dream blossom into life. At the zoo, the animal is the first client. Then comes the public, and then come the keepers and crews that maintain the exhibit. It seems to me to be the right order of things.

Soon the exhibit will be finished and open to all. When I am in this cool, damp canyon of luxurious shades of green, I sense that beneath my feet is good medicine for thousands of people. Our days slowly stretch towards summer when thousands of visitors will stream through the entry gates each day and head down this trail. By the end of my shift it will take all I have to smile at yet another person and point them on their way, but I will be stronger by then. My back, my biceps, and my commitment to this place will have strengthened and grown. The completed exhibit will seem smaller to me because I will have touched almost every tree and fabricated stone. Still, I have faith that Eagle Canyon will be spacious enough to hold the past, present, and future. If T.S. Eliot were here, we could walk together awhile. At the end of all our exploring, we'd arrive where we started and know the place for the very first time.

The Whitening of Winter

The backs of my knees are warm and vibrate. I have one of my housecats to thank for that, since he nestles against me and purrs before I get up in the morning. The dog groans and grumbles, stretches, and sets off down the hall, toenails clicking. I stumble behind her and when I give her the first pat of the day, I notice her fur is cool to the touch. There's a decided chill to the house and an absence of traffic noises outside. This is odd. I look to the window and what reflects back in shimmering waves of light, is SNOW!

Snow is magic to me — how it feels, how it looks, how it transforms the familiar into a new and enchanting place. It's like spun sugar, pixie dust, fairy sprinkles, and I want to taste it! I grew up on Southern California asphalt and spent most of my adulthood in the Arizona desert, so this cold fluffy stuff is a novelty for sure. I ignore the "clunk" of the dog banging her plastic food bowl on the linoleum in hopes of breakfast, and head to the closet for clothes and boots. I burst outside to the garden with the dog on my heels, and enjoy the satisfying crunch of frozen puddles and crusty snow.

I have a morning appointment at the zoo that I am determined to make. The radio stations unanimously call the weather "ugly", but I see only beauty. I decide to take the back roads, not realizing the snow there is three times deeper and has not yet met up with a snowplow. Slipping and sliding, I steer the car up the hills and slither down the dales. I crawl pass an accident that might have included me just minutes ago. I gingerly edge past a city bus that has slid into a snow bank. I plow pass entrances to the zoo parking lot that are pristine and impassable from their blanket of heavy fluff. Finally I head to my accustomed parking spot and drive my car forward, hard, using momentum to dig through the mounds of white and ease up to the curb.

There are no visitors today — it's early yet — and I have the place almost to myself. I have some time before the meeting so I head out for a lap around the zoo. My boots are silent in the deep powder. As I sink to my ankles, I think of elephants. They, too, are big and heavy against the miniscule six-pointed snowflakes that number in the millions as they make up these powdery mounds. Elephant feet are designed to move stealthily and silently with hardly a sound. What do they think of this morning's surprise? I reach the elephant barn and hear them inside, but it is not safe for these tropical natives to venture into a Northwest winter.

Disappointed at having missed my giant friends, I head towards the Arctic Tundra exhibit, wanting to see the animals that are native to this world of whiteness. From deep within, is there a surge of well-being and a feeling of "rightness" as the arctic creatures find their habitat covered in a white and woolly blanket? Do they hear ancient sounds of migrating birds and bellowing elk, now that normal zoo sounds of children's laughter and the hum of work trucks are silenced? Do they see the corners of their exhibit softened and cradled by a drift, and nestle under conifers and bare-twigged shrubs bowed down by thick clots of snow?

The snowy owl exhibit is before me, snowy, silent and cold. The foliage is covered. The rocks are snow-capped. Drifts of crystals sift down from the ledge above. It looks like a postcard or a painting with all distractions of angle or color or busyness erased. Nowhere is there a scrap of food from last night's feeding, or a bit of gum wrapper that might have blown in on the wind. My eyes slide over the unfamiliar setting looking for landmarks of what was there before the big chill. As my gaze passes over a second time, I blink. There, before me, is the snowy owl.

She is beautiful beyond words. The stunning white of her plumage blends in with the freshly fallen snow. Black ribbing patterns across her chest mimic the black of the boughs and slivers of rock that show through their hats of snow. Her eyes are motionless, staring back at me. Moments pass in near silence with only the sluggish drip, drip, drip of slowly melting ice to count out the time. That scene will be forever in my mind. It is in this unprecedented winter storm that the true nature of the animals can come forth. There are no distractions of people, sounds, or activity. It's just the simple cameo of an animal and an arctic landscape that gives us a flash of her essence in her natural world. The accustomed backdrop has changed so we are not lulled into a stupor of taking the scene for granted. Instead, it is new, fresh, and vital.

I share whispered words with a volunteer who passes by, camera gear in hand. It seems appropriate that she is shooting pictures — something that takes nothing from an animal except a split second of his privacy. It's also appropriate that we talk in hushed tones, not wanting to spoil the mood of the morning nor have noise sully an otherworldly experience of pristine cold, virgin white and stillness.

Staff from the veterinary clinic and the keepers are almost the only ones around. It's all about the animals now. Who is in the barn, sheltered and cared for, and who gets to go out? The ones out on exhibit are native to the area or from colder climes but many animals are kept in today. It reminds me again of how much geographic diversity we have on these grounds. There are rules and procedures in place to protect our more exotic inhabitants that are new to our climate. Hippos' ears will get frostbite if temperatures plunge. Their bodies are ungainly on land and a slip on an icy patch could cause a bruise or a break. An indoor heated pool steams warmly in the hippo barn, and our two hippos bob and sink in watery bliss.

Birds of prey housed in the mews sidle up to heat lamps turned on "high" and some targeted species get quickly transported to more sheltered indoor locations. The birds are usually in semi-indoor exhibits but wire mesh on one side opens up to the forest and the cold fingers of winter that seep in cause temperatures to plummet. An owl holds a dead mouse in his beak and hoots into the snowy wilderness, hoping to attract a wild mate with his gift. A Harris hawk from the Sonoran Desert huddles by his heat lamp, head under his wing, perhaps unsure of a world that has changed into unrecognizable drifts.

Elephants move restlessly indoors while keepers hover anxiously. Ever sensitive to sounds, their mighty ears can hear noises five miles away. The hush of traffic on the interstate and the absence of zoo visitors as the morning lengthens are unsettling to them. The sound of snow-movers on the grounds have them nodding heads, wagging ears, and moving restlessly as their huge brains process the information and go back through the years of memory to find a match. It's true that elephants never forget. Two of our herd are over 30 years old and have experienced heavy snow before. The keepers will not let them out onto the treacherous sloping yard that is now filled with snow and soon a crust of ice. If an elephant went down, no lift or crane is available to hoist 12,000 pounds upright! Yet heavy animals also need to move around or risk sore legs and feet. Add to that the mental stimulation that elephants require and the keepers have their hands full interacting with the herd and keeping them entertained while under house arrest of undetermined duration.

New animals that have never seen snow are watched carefully when they are let out of their "bedrooms" and into their exhibits. Orangutans who get a load of snow brought into their enclosure test, toss, and taste the grainy particles as they turn to ice in their hands and then melt away. Mountain goats leap nimbly through the drifts and across the rocks, hoof prints marking their jubilant exploration of their new world. Musk oxen stroll out in stately splendor, long hair looking like a fur coat on a matron going to the opera. Animals that don't know snow are less amused. Brows furrow, mouths pucker, feathers and fur fluff and shiver, and eyes dart from snow to keeper door and back again. Anything new is a potential threat to most creatures. Anxious or panicked animals are soothed and closely monitored as they explore this new world of shivering whiteness.

Green boa constrictors curl leisurely on their branch under the heat lamp, oblivious to the climactic wonder outside. Our slender-snouted crocodiles float dreamlessly in their indoor pool that is kept steady at a tepid 80-degrees. Tropical fish flit in their tanks. Mole rats scurry industriously in their heated burrows. Education program animals like the hedgehog and ferret rest easily in hutches and cages with warm bedding and thermostat-controlled heating. Today, I make no detours to admire them. The real excitement is outside. It's been 30 years since Portland has had a blanket of snow this spectacular. It is not to be missed!

I wander past the frosty glass of the tropical aviary and head down another path. What will I find? Water now runs darkly in the streams and pools as I pick my way through a black-and-white world. In the African Savannah, will zebras appear as black rippling ribbons suspended in a sea of white? Will the Arctic polar bears disappear, holding a paw over their face as in the wild to keep their wet black noses from showing? In Asia, what will the Siberian tigers think of the weather? When the snow begins to melt, will their paw prints seem to grow larger leaving enormous predator prints behind? What will the curious primates think when water that once flowed has turned to slush, and leaves that were once there for foraging are now covered with ice? I go forward to see.

The paths are treacherous and I look down to navigate safely. Staff have been clearing the paths for over three hours. I see a pair of workers, pink-cheeked and breathless, scraping with snow shovels to carve out a path for humans. Small riding tractors with scoops churn through the snow, piling it high to each side on the main thoroughfares. I'm going to new territory though, pristine and clear, like a new sheet stretched loosely over a soft mattress. Before me, I see the skittering trail of a light-footed field mouse. Further on are mid-sized bird tracks from migrating Canada Geese. Further still are deep claw marks from our resident peacocks and peahens. I spy a pair nearby, anxiously pecking into the snow looking for seeds or the answer to the conundrum of snow. I pause for a breath and look at the lacework of animal trails around me. These prints let me know about non-human "zoo visitors" — birds, rodents, and maybe even a weighty insect or two. Inches below are the concrete paths and wooden decks which we have introduced to this piece of Northwest forest. Today, and only today, we are reminded of the wild land on which it all began. Once again, Mother Nature reigns supreme.

After an hour of exploring in this winter world, I make my way back up to the entrance. Foliage bends over and tickles my face. I crouch and stumble through a tunnel of boughs. Clods of snow slip through the leafy fingers. Some skitters on my coat and down my neck, melting instantly on my warm skin. The secret hideout and the icy fingers of melting snow take me back to the excitement of kids making snow angels, leaping and laughing, and playing with the wonderment of it all. I see the plants in a new way, too. The landscape is no longer tame and controlled, cut back and pruned to not "get in the way." On this winter day the plants are unleashed and wild, weaving new arrangements as they hold up younger saplings that have been bent against them under a burden of snow. One old oak has cracked at the trunk and has fallen slowly to the ground. It is already partially covered with a shroud of whiteness, as it is laid to rest. The flora that shades, shelters, entertains and feeds the animals shows another face as it is transformed by winter. The snow brings me a new awareness of the part it plays in an animal's habitat.

I head to Steller Cove on my way out. It's the home of the Steller sea lion pair and our baby elephant seal. They are not on exhibit, though surely it is not too cold for them. Aren't they found in the north where arctic storms whip down the coast during the winter months? It is still, too still. The untouched blanket of white softens into translucent gray where the water of the pool laps its edges. Steam of sorts rises up from the pool as the dark water greets the cold air. The recording of barking sea lions echoes off the gunnite walls and snowy drifts in their exhibit. I feel a chill course through my body that's not from the cold of the day. I move closer to the exhibit for a better look, wrapping my coat tightly around me. Is something amiss? I warm my stiff cold hands with my breath and scan the area looking for signs of life.

Moments pass and I begin to feel anxious and unsettled. The silence is ominous; the lack of life seems unnatural. What if this was a real stretch of coastline and not an exhibit in a zoo? What if the animals were all gone, not just out of sight in a pool off-exhibit where they are safe and attended to? This is the silence of extinction; the absence of life as we have known it and have often taken it for granted. A quiet breeze steals up and I tighten my scarf and jam mittened hands into my deep pockets. Snow is beginning to melt. I stand there, nose starting to drip and feet cold and stiff. A slab of snow slithers off an educational plaque, exposing the warning sign: *Endangered Species.*

The zoo grounds are deserted. The sprinkling of early-morning staff and visitors have long since gone back to offices and cars. I am left alone with my thoughts and an empty replica of a coastal cove. The water swirls sluggishly in the cold. The little warmth of my breath vaporizes when it hits the chilled air. I scan the exhibit again and crane my head for a better look. I think I see movement! I edge to the corner of the viewing area, wedge my shoulder against the rock wall, and lean over to peer around a ledge in the pool. A wisp of vapor curls up, so faint that I might have imagined it. A timeless moment later, I see another wisp, spiraling up. I see her at last — a gray buoy bobbing in the water with thick wrinkled neck supporting her inquisitive head with dark sightless eyes and bristly whiskers. It is Mira, our baby elephant seal. Born with underdeveloped retinas, she has been sightless from birth. A rescue operation found her starving and almost dead. The Oregon Zoo took her, nursed her back to health, and is training her with auditory cues so she can respond to the keepers. I beam with the smile that parents reserve when gazing down at their infant. She is cute and luminous. She is my symbol that good things happen. There is hope that our endangered species can be saved.

Only a few of us witnessed this snowy day at the Oregon Zoo. A handful of photographers came for the love of art — catching that unique picture. Keepers came to keep their charges warm and safe. A handful of zoo visitors came to see their favorite place decked out in winter splendor. I came to see what I could see and learn what I could learn in this whitening of winter. The snowy day helped me take out the extraneous and put perspective back where it should be — on the safekeeping of the animals that call this zoo their home.

I trudged up the slope to the exit gates, cold, tired, but somehow warmed by the beauty of the snow and the miracle of Mira. As I began to wonder when the snow would disappear, the same thought came to me about the animals. When would they too disappear? The threat of extinction for many species in this zoo is measured in the years of my lifetime. I can't help but be deeply and personally affected. I don't want this to be the last glimpse — a final season of winter. I want them to be here in all the seasons and for lifetimes to come.

A Trunk-full of Knowledge

By definition, a zoo is "a museum with a living collection." People come to the zoo to have fun, but quite frankly, we're also in the business of education. To have captive animals for entertainment is not enough. They need to serve a purpose beyond that so we let education send a clear and urgent message about appreciation and conservation.

Did you know that one third of the U.S. population will visit a zoo at least once in a given year? Would you guess that the average zoo-goer is a woman under 30 years old with children? She's been to college but she'll walk right by the educational signs. On average, she and the kids will spend less than a minute at each exhibit unless there are baby animals or some sort of captivating activity that catches their eye.

All over town, hundreds of people pile into their cars to head for the zoo. Crowds number 10,000 or more on a summer day, spill into the overflow parking areas, and form long lines at the entrance and concession stands. People-watching is just as much fun as leaning over the railings to look at the animals, and for many families, the summer is not complete without frequent visits to the zoo. We know the zoo as a place with excited crowds, popcorn to munch, and souvenirs to buy and take home to shelve along with our memories. There are farm animals to pet, exotic animals to marvel over, and native animals who live in this region but we have never seen in the wild.

Most of the families will take a stroll by *Elephas maximus*, the Asian elephant. Kids are familiar with Jumbo, Babar, Dumbo, and Kipling's Elephant Child from books and TV. They now want to see the real thing. They want a look at the largest land mammal in the world. The trunk alone is heavier than them, mom, and dad put together! Anything that weighs as much as a school bus is something to see. Size counts for big points and larger animals are the most frequently visited at zoos.

It's winter now, and the zoo's school education programs are in full swing. I'm helping with an "Elephant Encounter" for an out-of-town group and check my watch. The bus should be arriving by now and fifteen sixth-graders will be piling out after an hour-long ride that has left them antsy and twitching. They are in high spirits. Who wouldn't trade a day indoors in an over-crowded classroom for a Friday of freedom and adventure at the zoo? It's winter and cold outside but the rain is waiting until later. The elephants are contentedly roaming around the yard and the other volunteers and I all turn as one when we hear the tumult.

A flood of pre-teens in coats and parkas come laughing down the path, the boys pushing and shoving, the girls giggling and nudging. Pet, the matriarch of the elephant cows, turns her massive head to assess the group. Shine and Rose-Tu follow her lead and ponderously swings around to look. Little Chendra lollygags at the pool before lumbering over to see what the commotion is all about.

The teacher beckons us out of earshot of the kids and talks with us in hushed tones. "I hope these kids can connect with these animals. They have a really short attention span and don't seem to recall what they've just learned. In class it's all I can do to just keep their attention."

We listen and nod our heads. Kids need to experience first, talk later. They won't forget a direct experience and in that way, make their own personal connection. Don't ask them how many toes are on the front and back feet of an Asian elephant because they won't remember. What they'll tell their friends about in spectacular detail is what happened when the elephant stepped on a watermelon or when he pooped. I can hear it now: "Yuck! His poop is the size of a basketball! And didja know — it weighs up to 25 pounds!" Small children, especially boys, are fascinated with the bodily functions of all our animals. I find myself amazed as well. Twenty-five pounds? Imagine that!

Kids also want you to be an enthusiastic fellow-adventurer. Whether you are a parent, staff person or volunteer, children will tug on your coat sleeves until you come along to have fun with them. I'm on deck first, so I get everything going. Making a megaphone out of my hands, I call out to the wriggling mass of kids. "Elephant training time! Everyone down to the concert lawn, on the double!" I take off like a shot, running past their shocked faces and down the path to the lawn. In my red shirt I'm hard to miss, and the chaperones herd the kids and follow the stampede in hot pursuit. Panting, we all gather on the lawn.

One of my little known skills is the ability to imitate various wild animals so I let loose an elephant bellow that snaps their heads forward and it quiets the group in record time. "Now that I have your attention," I say demurely but with a grin. "Let's begin. The first order of business in training an elephant is to tell him to stop immediately and don't move. The command is 'STEADY.' Another useful command is 'MOVE UP.' It means to move forward. Everyone got that?" All the kids nod vigorously, wide-eyed. This adventure is more fun than expected!

"Let's go then," I said. "You're the elephants, I'm the trainer. Anyone who makes a mistake doesn't get any peanuts." I could see those little minds whirling. Most kids are hungry just moments after finishing their latest meal. I knew the bus ride and the proximity to the noon hour would work in my favor. "MOVE UP" I shout, and start a brisk walk across the wide expanse of lawn. A quick glance over my shoulder shows that the group is following. We circle round in figure eights, leap over concrete benches, weave around trees, and climb rapidly up and down gentle slopes of lawn.

We practice being elephants in other ways, too. A group of us simulate the daily migration in search of food, brushing against the tickling tips of bamboo which sway in the breeze. We search for water and gulp cool draughts from the drinking fountain or lean over the elephant enclosure railing and strain to reach the pool with our make-believe "trunks." Our activities pique the curiosity of one of the cows and she interrupts her dust bath to stare at us. With a snort she resumes, curling her trunk around some sand, tossing it over her head to her back and sending a fine mist of dust over half the kids. The moms will have more laundry challenges when the tired kids come home, but the kids will have been touched by some elephantine fairy dust while watching her daily bathing ritual.

Over the next 15 minutes I teach them a few of the universal elephant trainers' commands: KNEEL means to place both front knees on the ground. LAY DOWN directs them to lie down on one side. FOOT is to raise a foot. TRUNK is the favorite, as they make trunks out of their clasped hands and straightened arms. When they start trunk-wars, I know it is time to change the venue.

Calisthenics are next and we assemble in rows. Coats and scarves are flung to the ground. Red-cheeked smiles show me the kids are warming up to this experience, literally and figuratively. Sit-ups are first and the group looks like insects flipped over with waving hands and feet. Headstands are next with lots of giggles and body slams. We end with people-pyramids and as the 130-pound heavyweight of my particular group, I am unfortunately part of the bottom tier. My shoulder buckles under the knee of a husky youngster the next level up but I visualize the strong pillar-like leg of an elephant and am able to bear the weight for another moment. Our pyramid abruptly crumbles into a mass of squirming bodies and the exercise is over. The elephant cows watch us with bemused expressions. The kids sneak furtive peaks at them from time to time. They love the time to roughhouse but I can tell that they want to see what the elephants can do!

We play on the lawn a while longer but finally I gather the troops. I'm starting to feel winded, despite my regular workouts at the gym. Surely those kids must be tiring too? "STEADY" I shout, stopping in my tracks. A few students domino against one another but in general the mass comes to a shuddering halt. "MOVE UP" I shout again and we're off. We line everyone up linking hands and pretending that we're trunk-to-tail with the one in front of us. That brings us back to the elephant area and I shout "STEADY" for the last time. We have a renewed appreciation for the strength, coordination, and agility that the elephants need when we see the routines that they will do next. We also have a collection of sneaker-prints on our backs and shoulders and grass stains on our knees, as merit badges for our efforts.

Laughing and panting, the kids line up to get their snacks, just like the elephant cows are asked to line up for a training session. A serpentine line of giggling kids crunch on peanuts from their snack bags and tromp up the winding path to the overlook. Four elephants are rocking back and forth on massive feet in anticipation. June, the head elephant keeper, is ready to speak.

"These are our four female elephants," June says with a proud smile. We watch three keepers enter the area to the delight of the animals. "Pet, Shine, Rose-Tu, and Chendra are their names." She explains that the keepers spend about a third of their time training and teaching the animals which keeps the herd mentally stimulated and physically exercised.

The kids watch with fascination as the keepers direct the animals to lift a foot, lift their trunk, open their mouth, kneel down, lie on their sides, and sit on a platform and raise their front legs in the air. Rose-Tu is the smart one and walks carefully across a log balanced on two strong supports. Pet's arthritis is acting up and she is moving slower than usual. Shine plays off her and is initially reluctant to go through her repertoire of commands with precision. June teases and cajoles her. Soon Shine is in the spirit of the game and her inherent sweetness comes through. Chendra is happy-go-lucky as always, and cute as a button. She skips when she runs and is an instant favorite of the children since she is so small and playful.

The elephants' finale is to create a pyramid with Shine hunkering down and Pet and Rose-Tu putting their forefeet on her back! I wince and roll my right shoulder where I can feel a slight bruise forming from the antics with the kids. "Two tiers high, 65-80 pounds apiece...." I do the mental calculation of the squirming bodies that were standing on my back and know the elephants have an easier time of it, pound-for-pound. The kids are paying rapt attention because they've been doing the exact same activities.

The group splits up now for an exercise called "Silent Observation." I motion five youngsters to come with me and we go to the indoor viewing area. Rama is there for us to observe. We take out our pads and pencils and find a spot along the glass. I hand the paper to a student named Emily, who shyly reads us the rules: "Elephants have much to teach us. Watch the animal for five minutes and write down what you see. Then there will be time for discussion. End the session by watching in silence for five more minutes, to see if you see things in a different way." She smiles nervously up at me and chews on her lower lip.

"What if he doesn't move or anything?" she says earnestly. "What do we write then?" "That's a good question," I return. "What do you think?" "Well," she considers, "maybe we can write what his skin looks like or his toes." "That would be fine," I say. "The more carefully you look, the more you'll notice. Now is everyone ready to start? Remember, no more talking once we start, until five minutes are up."

A voice comes from the back of the group. "What if we run out of things to write?" A boy named Drew drums his pencil against the bench, a dynamo of energy that is reluctant to sit still. "Well," I respond with a lifted brow, "how about using your imagination?" Drew considers this and an idea forms in his mind. He trains his eyes on the elephant and readies his pencil on the pad. Armando is tapping his foot impatiently, holding the stopwatch and ready to press the plunger to start the time. I nod to him and the clock starts ticking. Heads drop to their notebooks and the kids start writing.

Rama is in musth. Fluid leaks from the temporal glands on the sides of his face. Urine darkens the gray leathery skin on his back legs. He is restlessly flapping his ears and pacing back and forth. He doesn't look at us but instead, peers at the inner door or the concrete wall as he treads heavily up and back. I listen hard and can hear the muffled sound of his steps, the raspy scratch of his legs as the skin rubs against skin, and the moist whoosh of his breath. I can hear Packy in the distance, butting his head against the metal doors and sounding like a cannon. If I strained, I might even hear sounds from the cows in the far yard, walking quietly across the sand or pulling long stalks of bamboo from under the service gate.

Five minutes pass in a flash for me because I am thinking up new elephant stories to write, musing about Rama's brain function, and noticing how the wrinkles in his skin look texturally like a faux finish I've been planning for my bathroom. The kids' minds are busy too, clicking away. It's always amazing to see a group of children so still, wrapped up in their own thoughts and ideas. Pencils scrawl across pads. Eyes stare from faces open-mouthed with wonder. Heads follow Rama's pacing like an audience at a tennis match, back-and-forth, back-and-forth. Armando's timer goes off with a PING! We are all startled out of our thinking and lists.

Our discussion takes off with gusto. What did you see? Big, gray, bald. Then more detailed descriptions: kind eyes, shiny toenails, tail like a giraffe, long eyelashes. Kids start relating them to their own physiology: cracked and leathery and needs lotion, loose skin like he's old, humpbacked, bald, firehouse trunk. Finally, they relate him to things they see in their environment or on TV: bigger than our school bus, like a war tank, like a living statue. Ideas ignite more ideas. Lists are added to as new observations are called out. The discussion skyrockets out of control and I step back to let the kids shout and try to best each other with great ideas. I think back to a famous educator who invites us to see education as "provocation," not mere instruction. I cannot tell the children what an elephant is and, even if I tried, I couldn't match the richness of their experience of discovery that happens in these past few minutes.

We do our last five-minute observation to see what the elephant is doing. I know he is in musth and is expressing an excess of physical and sexual energy. The kids see a wider rainbow of possibilities. He's marching, singing, calling to his baby, talking to someone in the wall, wanting to bugle, looking for carrots, or dancing. He's scared that mice will come in and he wants to come out from behind the glass and be with us. These are great observations because they have delved into Rama's psyche to guess what's going on in his thoughts and with his emotions. Kids are open to all possibilities. They easily cross the line that separates animal and man, and accept without question that elephants might share our human urges for self-expression, the need to connect, and to entertain fears. A trained school psychologist would have a field day if we took this exercise deeper. What issues and angst are mirrored in the students' observations? What positive indicators of compassion, social adjustment, and identity formation are apparent as they relate to another life form? The kids wail when the timer goes off this time, wanting to write more. It's only the lure of lunch that pulls them away and we join the other groups outdoors.

We're back on the concert lawn and I lay under a tree, hands under my head. My uniform is wrinkled. My pad is full of notes. My mind is buzzing with elephant wonder. I'm pleasantly tired and satisfied with what we've seen and done this morning. We've had fun but we've also learned. A zoo staffer is supervising the lunch activities and I am off-duty, at least for the next half hour. I watch Peter and Camilla pillage each other's lunch bags, trading cookies for chips and feeling like they each got the better part of the deal. I see Miyoko delicately eating rice and bento with chopsticks. There's Javier wolfing down a burrito and hardly chewing. The feeding frenzy is fun to watch and I can't help but relate it to feeding time in the elephant barn.

I sit up to dig into my lunch bag and munch on sticks of raw carrot, a favorite of mine. Our elephants also have decided preferences. Some will eat carrots before apples. Others prefer sweet potatoes over carrots. Peter and Camilla could relate to that. Miyoko and her deft use of chopsticks make her the envy of her classmates, but do they know that these elephants can pick up sunflower seeds or a 1,000-pound log with equal facility with their prehensile trunks? Javier's mom always tells him to slow down and chew, but he doesn't listen. Elephants might be better in the chewing department with their four 10-

pound molars, but they only digest 30% of what they eat and pass the rest out for the keepers to pick up.

As I'm eating my own salad that fits in a mid-sized plastic container, I think of the massive amounts of browse that the elephants eat. Packy is the larger male elephant at the zoo, and at 13,000 pounds is one of the largest Asian elephants in North America. As a mega-herbivore, I am astonished by the fact that if he were in the wild, he could eat 500 pounds of foliage in a given day! He would easily stroll down to the Willamette River, five miles to the east, browsing as he went. Then he could swim across, lingering there if it was a warm day. Onward he'd go, to the airport and beyond. Walking over 50 miles and browsing 16 hours or more would be all in a day's work for him in the wild. Life at the zoo is much more tame. A few miles in a day is considered good, and browsing from piles of collected hay, bamboo, fruits and vegetables is easy pickings.

The kids have finished their meal and are in a circle at the feet of one of the volunteer animal interpretive guides. He is telling them about how elephants learn. The elephant brain is an amazing thing. At birth, most animals' brains are 90% developed, leaving them 10% to learn new things. Much of their behavior, therefore, is based on primitive instinct and reaction without much conscious thought in between. The elephant brain is 35% formed at birth, leaving them with lots of room for adaptability and higher learning later in life. Studies on human brains have shown that the Einsteins among us have more convolutions, creating more brain surface in which to store information. The elephant brain is four-and-a-half times larger than ours and is more convoluted. Hm... who might be learning from whom?

The kids pay rapt attention to the volunteer since he is charismatic and enthusiastic, but what if they sat in a row behind Pet, the matriarch of our little herd? She's older than their parents and her memory is better. Her privileged place in an elephant family means she can teach about the importance of strong familial ties. Statistically, about half of these kids are from single-parent households or have been adopted by a stepparent. Learning how elephant herds create and depend on a strong social structure with a focus on teaching and passing on knowledge could bring new understanding to these children's lives.

Stories tell of the elephants' instinctive loyalty to the group. In times of danger, adults will surround the calves in a protective circle facing out toward the enemy. Other species will cut and run much sooner when danger threatens. Perhaps children can learn from this too. That confronting the class bully as a group is a better way to deal with disagreements than running. Domestic elephants also seem to have a longing to put in a day's work to get a day's food. Don't children also strive to do well in school for the praise of their parents and ultimately, for that feel-good feeling that comes from a job well done? With the role model of an elephant, more cars might sport the bumper sticker: "My student is an honor student at _____ school!"

The Elephant Encounter continues as the kids file into a classroom to handle the elephant biofacts up close. I hand Tony a ten-pound molar that has been grinding foliage for decades before being shed for a new one. "Elephants can have six sets of teeth over their lifetime," I explain, "and the new ones just come moving down from the back of the jaw and push out the old ones." Tony looks silently on. I see him slip his tongue to one of his own teeth. The light goes on and he relates his two sets of teeth to the fascinating multiplicity of elephant molars.

Charlie rummages through a rubber tub and draws out a Frisbee-sized disc of horny material. "What's this?" he asks me. I answer by pulling out farriers' tools from the box, along with other foot-trimming equipment. We lay them all out with a diagram of an elephant's foot and start comparing horse shoeing with elephant pedicure procedures. Charlie lives in the country with horses so the elephant is a little less of a mystery but even more of a miracle.

Sara and Paula are inquisitive and are poking around in the items on a sturdy wheeled cart. I come over to help and together, we carefully lift off a massive femur bone. We hold the bone up to our own femurs, the leg bone that goes from hip to knee. As we stand in a row, they can see how their small bones will grow to adult-size ones like mine. It would take more than twice our height to be as tall as an elephant and grow into the gargantuan bone I've balanced on its end. Knowing comes from association. Now they know how their thigh and my thigh and an elephant's thigh relate to each other.

It's time to wrap up the day and the kids file back into the indoor viewing area for a last goodbye to Packy, who is rolling his metal food drum and using his trunk to blow Cheerios into his mouth for an afternoon snack. Trunks are good for practical jokes, too. A keeper offers him a plastic zoo cup filled with water and Packy takes a long draught with his trunk. In a flash, he flings his trunk towards us and shoots the water out, making us jump back as it splashes across the glass. His gentle eye twinkles back at us as it has at zoo visitors for over 40 years.

The kids gather coats and caps and head back to the bus. Their minds are churning, thinking about elephant gymnastics that they'll practice on the living room floor after dinner. At night, they'll lie under flannel sheets and warm quilts and imagine what elephants might dream about. As they reach into their lunch bags tomorrow at school, they might have a renewed interest in fruits and vegetables when they realize it is a food they share with these gentle giants. When running, they might notice their femurs; when chewing, their molars. How similar elephants are to us in their physiology, yet on an entirely different scale.

The peals of laughter dim as the group disappears up the path. As I go to the viewing area to collect my papers and coat, their chatter seems to echo warm and bright in the concrete room. I pause to notice the fragrance of timothy hay and elephant scent, and strain to hear the rumble of an elephantine voice too low for me to hear. Today we've had a lot of fun, but have also gained a trunk-full of knowledge. Rama is standing quietly in the center of the room and lifts his trunk in a drowsy salute as I turn to leave. His long lashes sweep over his gentle eyes and he bobs his head once, before settling down into a half-sleep.

Which is More Precious?

About the time my parents were born, a dozen mountain goats were transported from Alaska and Canada to the Olympic Mountains in Washington State. The goats were stocked in the area for hunters. One human generation later, hundreds of their descendents have seriously damaged the ecosystem of plants and soils by grazing, trampling and wallowing. Ultimately, which is more precious? Is it the mountain goat? The hunters? Or is it a collection of plants, soils, and animals that had first rights to that land from millennium before?

Should we hunt down the goats in order to restore the balance of nature and hope that the land eventually returns to what it once was? Animal activists bristle. Why should these regal animals suffer through no fault of their own? Ecologists rub their chins and ponder. Removal may make sense. Goats have taken food originally meant for other species, skewing the numbers and types of animals that exist in the Olympics in a way that was new to the region. Hunters stand divided. Many have a strong ecological bent and want to see animal populations monitored and controlled by the number of hunting tags issued. Others might enjoy the idea of easy pickin's since mountain goats are much more scarce and elusive in their native environment. But what do *I* think? I wander to the zoo on a bright spring day, and wonder....

I've written Webster's definition of "precious" in my notebook. It reads: *"Of great value or high price, highly esteemed or cherished."* On the lookout for a story, I'm swept up with a laughing tide of zoo visitors. I end up in the primate area and look around for preciousness. I've always had a secret wish to cradle a baby orangutan in my arms. Is it a latent and too-late yearning for motherhood, or my female predilection for nurturing? I don't know. I imagine that the baby would be heavy in my arms. Her leathery skin would be softer than I had expected. The wispy orange hair would be coarser. The chocolate eyes staring up at me would be the windows to an enigmatic soul that I'd want to get to know better.

The reality of glass between us is before me, protecting the animals from coughs and colds of the crowd, and protecting us from curious primate hands and projectiles of food and feces. We have to settle for looking, not touching. I squat down with a group of kids to peer out at Inji and her grandson Kutai. I help a young girl unpack her backpack and show Kutai her comb, sunglasses and a small hand mirror. Kutai sits with one hand across his lap and another under his chin, following the girl's every moment with café-au-lait eyes and an intelligent expression. Inji moves towards a toddler who pats the glass that separates them. The toddler leans forward and kisses the glass. Inji steps up and quickly kisses him back. The crowd is delighted!

I move back to let another layer of curious people forward. They squat down to be eye-to-eye with the orangs and I watch their excited interactions. This is why visitor surveys and books on zoo management say that the animals most visited are the ones most like us — the monkeys and apes. We can relate to them because they look like us and have similar behaviors.

I idly scratch my arm and notice tiny red marks along its length. It's from a Philippine sailfin lizard that I held yesterday in a reptile handling class. I had strapped him into his tiny harness and leash for safekeeping, lifted him to my arm, and then transferred him into his carrier. He clung to my warm forearm in cold-blooded affection, the sharp scales of his underbody pricking my sensitive skin.

He was spectacular to behold: sailfins on his back, multi-colored skin, long graceful toes and pointed nails, and a watchful and stalwart countenance. The oddity of a third eye or pineal eye on his head makes him extra-special. It's a light detector that is thought to be a homing mechanism. But who is more precious? A cuddly primate that looks like the baby I never had, or an amazing scaly creature that abrades my skin and has three eyes?

I roam on in my search to define and decide which is most precious. There are over 200 species and 1300 individual animals at this zoo. I pass by elephants, giraffes, tigers, and an elephant seal and hum the popular refrain that says it all: *"Lions, tigers, and bears, oh my!"* We are attracted to the big animals and they are deemed more precious by us when fundraising events are held. They garner the most donations, are adopted by more "ZooParents," star in the most photos of hundreds of amateur photographers, and are printed on stacks of tee shirts of all sizes.

I must admit I'm impressed by Packy, our largest bull elephant, and make an effort to see him every time I'm at the zoo. Touted as being one of the biggest Asian elephants in North America, Packy makes the truck scales creak at 13,000 pounds! He eats almost 200 pounds of food a day. He and the gang each polish off a large part of three 25-pound sacks of carrots that gives new meaning to the admonition to "eat your vegetables!" Kids at zoo camp try to heft a carrot bag by themselves and stagger around the cold storage floor in disbelief.

We know the community values our elephants because more people turn out for Packy's birthday party than attend parties on behalf of local politicians or celebrities. The keepers want a pole feeder for the elephant yard so the herd can pull their timothy hay from up high, simulating foraging in the wild from trees in the Asian forests. I think about what's in my investment account and want to spring for that item on their behalf. It takes a lot of money to maintain the zoo, and people will pay for what they think is important.

A little known fact is that the popularity of the larger animals helps to fund the care and feeding of the smaller ones like tropical birds, endangered lizards, exotic fish, and small mammals. The most expensive animals to feed are not the elephants or rhinos that tilt the scales at thousands of pounds. No, it's the 60-pound sea otter that has an expensive diet of seafood including clams, squid and crab. Who is funding *his* meal plan that comes in at a hefty $40-60 per day?

As my mind circles around to calculate meal tickets for various animals in the zoo, I almost walk by the Western pond turtle habitat. The turtles are not big. We collect them when they're quite small in fact — the size of lunch for an invasive species, the bullfrog. Every summer, volunteers and conservation scientists go out into the field, collecting eggs or hatchling turtles to bring back to this safe place. At the zoo, the turtles grow and mature until they are too big of a mouthful for the bullfrog. Volunteers and staff head out again where the pond turtles were originally collected, and return them to live and breed. Grant money pays for this, but isn't it easier to provide creature comforts for our ever-popular elephants than sell the idea of increasing the numbers of some small reptiles that we may have never seen before?

What aspect of an animal will tug at our heartstrings and ignite us to take action or dip into our pocketbooks? Which is more precious, the large or the small?

I have a friend at the zoo who has a curious past and curious pets. She managed the menagerie at a circus, was a field biologist, trained and rode a zebra stallion, and is now a respected zoo volunteer. She told me about the mysteries of an animal and part of its life cycle the other day. The male and female call the rotting leaves under the trees of the lush humid rainforest their home. When mating time comes, they sniff each other out, meet, playfully groom each other, and then do an elaborate courtship dance together. The male creates a sperm sac that looks like a beautiful pearl and lovingly transfers it to the female. The female takes it in to fertilize her eggs and then scurries to find a perfect nesting area in a protected part of the forest floor. After laying her eggs, she vigilantly watches over them until they hatch out. She stays there and guards them in their first days of life. You may have never guessed but this is a foot-long millipede. Without her and others like her, we'd soon be drowning in detritus and plant debris. Isn't the millipede absolutely precious?

I wander by the Insect Zoo that is the unfortunate but necessary victim of the next budget cut. Expenses such as utility costs have soared so much that although the revenue at the gate is steadily increasing, there's just not enough money to go around. The wooden structure and the caged inhabitants of the

Insect Zoo may disappear, but the facts remain. Our food chain demands that little creatures at the bottom feed the bigger ones at the top. It takes thousands of aphids to feed a few larger insects that in turn feed a bird for an hour or a day. Dozens of bunnies feed a single hawk in a month and it takes many a deer, boar, and hare to keep a leopard alive for a year. Shouldn't the small and the plentiful be called precious because they support the large and magnificent that we swarm to the zoo to see?

I pass the Amur leopards next as I continue my stroll through the zoo. Frederick and Andrea lounge like big house cats on their heated rock, not realizing that at last count, only 39 of their relatives were left in the wild. By the time the infant that is peering at them applies to the college of his or her choice, this species of cats will almost certainly be extinct. The infant sucks tearfully on a pacifier as a new tooth begins to break through his gums. Nationwide, zoo staff gnaw on pencils, chew on gum, and take up smoking again as they nervously prepare to decide which of the species of large cats will be part of a nation-wide species conservation program and which will be allowed to go quietly, regrettably, and irrevocably extinct.

This animal has evolved for more than 4,000,000 years but in the last 100, poaching and habitat loss have just about wiped them out. There are only a few suitable breeding pairs, severely limited space at accredited zoos, and only a trickle of funding for cryogenic freezing in the hopes that later technology can resurrect animals that would have already disappeared from the planet. There is no time to lose. Which is more precious, the species in my zoo or the species in yours?

We share the planet with ten million other species. It doesn't take rocket science — just an average trip on a plane where you can look down — to show that *Homo sapiens* have taken up more than their share of space. Conservation biologists believe it may require 30-70% of untouched biosphere simply to maintain biodiversity. Currently, only about three percent is in protected parks or reserves. A large cryogenic freezer with digital display and high-tech monitors houses eggs and sperm that patiently await their future, whatever it is. This zoo is a shining gem in the midst of these statistics. Over 1,300 individual animals are protected, respected, studied and written about, as mankind decides where to put his time and money, and turn stewardship into an action verb.

I'll be flying from Oregon to Arizona tomorrow and will look out of the window through the sparkle of dawn to coastline, forest, desert, and urban sprawl. As is my custom, my luggage bulges with as many books as clothes. My mind is filled with thoughts to ponder and stories to write. As I visit other places and another zoo, I'll take the time to reflect. Which is more precious?

I know for certain that I want to have it all: the mountain goat and the mosses and clays of the Olympic Mountains; the baby orangutan that has fingers and toes like me, and the lizard with its third eye that can possibly see the world in a new way; the elephant which is the biggest land mammal, and the pond turtle that is small enough to be eaten by a frog with a single gulp; the creepy crawly insects as well as the animals they feed and the forests they decompose; and the leopard at both my zoo and the one I'll see this week. I go home to pack my suitcase, thinking of preciousness and all that I cherish. The words of American ecologist Aldo Leopold ring in my ears: "The first rule of intelligent tinkering is to save all the parts." Everything is precious. Let's try to save it all.

Above All Else, Be Kind

The hero is pining away on a tropical Hawaiian island after the loss of his love, in the romance novel I'm reading. His young daughter needs a woman's touch, so he advertises in the personal ads. Hundreds respond with perfumed letters citing their height, weight, and experience with children. The hero scans each floral sheet and writes back to the very few that interest him. He is no longer hoping for a forever love, but simply wants to raise his little girl with some sense of grace. His return letters ask what the applicants' childhood rearing philosophy is. The winner, who becomes the heroine of the story and of course his forever love, writes these simple words: "Children need a gentle hand and a warm heart. When in doubt, above all else, be kind."

An expression of kindness is the furthest thing from my mind when I enter the Amazon Flooded Forest exhibit, late one sultry morning in July. The animal and plant life in the exhibit replicates what we'd see in the wilds. Turtles, a caiman, and shimmering fish glide through sparkling clear water that draws you in, a nose-length from the glass. Our magnificent anaconda winds her way among the underwater roots of a tall tree. A soft red-brown agouti explores the luxurious underbrush for treats. Howler, tamarin, and saki monkeys scamper through the lush foliage, and a toucan springs from branch to branch showing off his brightly colored beak.

At precisely 11 a.m., Jesus Lopez opens a camouflaged door from behind a synthetic mangrove tree trunk. He can be heard through the loudspeaker that crackles and spits over the heads of dozens of clamoring children from Rhino Camp, resplendent in their matching spring-green tee shirts. We all press our noses to the glass, as Jesus moves slowly through the Amazon. In his hand is a stainless steel bowl full of chopped fruit and he tosses chunks to what we are told are fruit-eating fish. Judy, the agouti, lumbers over to him and gets a slice of ripe melon gently extended to her. The toucan bounces over as well, cocks a beady eye, clacks his beak, and is rewarded with a purple grape that he rolls back and forth in his beak before tossing it down with a gulp.

Jesus gives us facts and figures while more animals gather round. The monkeys are curious as cats, and dangle by hands and feet to see what's in the bowl for them. Jackie, our White-faced saki monkey, hangs by her prehensile tail and begins to run her fingers through Jesus' hair. This is a common grooming ritual amongst monkeys, and Jesus enjoys what he affectionately calls his "hair treatment." He hands up some choice morsels to her which she takes as her due, and moves carefully so as not to startle her. He turns to hand out treats to her mate, Bam Bam. Bam Bam is much more reticent, recovering from dental surgery and being intrinsically less trusting of humans. Jesus selects the softest bits of fruit and holds them out one by one, in a painstaking process. It is hot and humid in the exhibit and the sweat starts to bead and run down the keeper's temples, but he continues, patient and kind.

These little moments in time and compassionate actions tell the measure of a man. Like many employees, Jesus has been here for many years and still brings care and attention to scheduled tasks like feeding, cleaning, training, and doctoring that are needed every day. It would be easy to rush through the routine, brushing aside an inquisitive animal in the haste to get the job done, but keepers are here for the animals. Jesus comes out to our side of the glass once his interpretive talk is finished, and we have a one-on-one chat about the poison dart frogs. The frogs have been moved back on display from a holding area where they spent the winter. Thirty healthy jewel-like frogs have now dwindled to 16 and the unexplained mortality rate alarms the keepers. The keepers rearrange the exhibit foliage, rocks and gravel. They twiddle with the humidifier and heat lamps. They finally pick up the frogs, hold them in their palms, and look into the depths of their glossy amber eyes for answers. The zoo's excellent veterinary pathologist promises necropsy results in a day or two but I can tell that Jesus is deeply concerned. "It hurts," he says. "Even when it's just a frog or a fish that dies, it hurts. You're with them day in and day out and get to know them. When something like this happens, you feel it."

It's true, isn't it? The public won't miss a frog or two, but for the keeper, a life that is lost is no small tragedy. Exotic animal medicine is rife with uncertainty so when in doubt, above all else they try to be kind. They'll trek out to the keeper library and thumb through mountains of books. They'll make notes, share information with other zoos, and talk with their spouse about it over dinner at night.

I turn to leave and Jesus is setting out chopped fruit for Xavier and Fidget, the pygmy marmosets. Smaller than a handful, they prance down the limb and leap nimbly onto his shirt. They sit trustingly. I know that whatever disease or injury threatens their tiny lives, they will be carried by broad shoulders and will rest in kind hands.

Hours later I'm back at home. I sit at the computer, the blank screen mirroring my uninspired mind. I am tired after a busy day, slow-moving freeway traffic, and efforts to finish pieces of the flotsam and jetsam of modern life. Like Alice in Wonderland, I try to stride briskly forward but feel like I'm staggering further and further behind. I take a sip from my water glass, hoping the cat hasn't lapped from it while I was away. I flex my hands, lean forward and wait for inspiration. Moments pass. I unwrap a tiny brick of peppermint gum hoping the freshness will dance with my taste buds and wake up my brain. My gaze drifts to the wall calendar and I note the month and the day. A flood of memories come streaming back.

At another zoo, Tara was pregnant for the first time. Gestation in orangutans is about 250 days, but she had a miscarriage two months early. A premature scrap of an infant was born dead one night, barely three pounds but already covered with downy wisps of orange hair. The effect on Tara was profound. She hugged the shriveled corpse of her baby, trying in vain to make it suckle and whimpering in distress when it did not respond. She paced around the enclosure, swinging up to her nesting area and back down with the wrinkled fetus clutched to her chest.

The next morning, the nursery group was boisterous as Hera, Kali and Lilith played with their babies. Live, healthy little ones from newborn to two years old, crawled, scampered and leaped around the enclosure or interacted with their mothers. Tara sat alone in a corner, heartbroken. The morning keeper saw the tiny fetus and approached her but Tara would not give up the baby. Over the next several days, she lost weight alarmingly. She was listless, her eyes grew dull, and her fur was limp. She was ignored by the other females and didn't have the energy to groom herself. Ribs began to show as she picked disinterestedly at her food, and as the days went by, the keepers were more than alarmed.

The veterinarian mentioned Tara to Brigit, a middle-aged veterinary assistant who was new to the zoo. She listened intently and then marched out to go and see Tara. At the door of the isolation area where Tara was housed, Brigit pushed ahead to go in. The vet grabbed her arm and cautioned her not to go on. This was an orangutan that matched her pound-for-pound in weight, but had four times her strength. Tara was also in a disturbed and unpredictable mood. At last he relented, knowing that primates can take a shine to one person more than another. Brigit's petite frame and female gender might seem less threatening to the bereft orangutan.

Brigit went in crouched low, avoiding eye contact with Tara who sat facing the corner. Speaking in a quiet voice, Brigit squatted down by the door, apparently unconcerned, and started speaking in soothing tones. "What's the matter, love?" she murmured. "I know all about it. There, there now." She continued talking, prattling on and on about next to nothing. Tara sat stony-faced and disconsolate in the corner. Brigit continued talking. After several minutes, she stretched a leg out, then another, and sat down to lean against the wall. She gave a few looks into Tara's direction and continued talking in a singsong manner. "Everything is going to be OK, you'll see," she said. "Come on, give me your hand." On and on she talked until Tara cocked her head and seemed to be listening. It took another half hour until the orang made any eye contact. In another half hour, Tara sidled up to her and pressed a shaky forearm against Brigit's side, clutching the infant with the other hand. Brigit leaned into her, rocking back and forth. With blue medical scrubs touching long orange hairs, Brigit started singing a soft lullaby.

An hour later, Brigit was still cuddling Tara who had snuggled into her lap and put her broad lips to Brigit's shoulder. Brigit stroked her hair, keeping up the flow of sympathetic talk. Then, just like that, Tara gave her the dead baby. Brigit took it, cradled it, talked admiringly about it, and slipped it into the pocket of her smock. She offered Tara a small piece of ripe banana that was in a feeding tray nearby. After suspiciously examining the fruit and the slim fingers that held it, Tara allowed Brigit to hand feed her.

Brigit returned twice a day for the next week and Tara became decidedly more tranquil. Brigit talked to her like women do with their girlfriends, giving her lots of cuddles, laughing at this and that, and playing games with the fruit and monkey chow in the enclosure to keep Tara interested in eating again.

Within three weeks, Tara had started to feed herself and had gained back the weight she had lost.

Brigit had a story too, that she only shared with her closest friends. Perhaps her own inner journey would have been quicker and her healing more complete had she had someone who understood and comforted her. It could have very well been an animal — a household dog that would have had showered her with unconditional love every day that she came home from work. Or perhaps a horse that she had a special rapport with. Perhaps even an animal at the veterinary clinic at the zoo. Something as solid, wise, and long-lived as a tortoise could have given the strength she needed to endure. Perhaps a pack of wolf pups orphaned by their own mother would have given her an outlet for her own maternal instincts. Or perhaps saving the life of an injured bird of prey by assisting with a complex surgical procedure could give her the feeling that she had saved a life, not just lost one.

There are stories like this in every zoo. Some are chronicled and some are not. It might be the daily actions of a gentle keeper that are done with kindness and care, or a truly inspirational interaction with one animal that comes into your life at exactly the right moment. I wander through the grounds at times, resting my zoo-weary feet for a moment on benches that have memorial plaques. They honor kind people who have loved the zoo and who have had a hand in supporting it and making it a better place. The elephant house has terra cotta bricks in the wall with sculpted peacocks and tigers and rhinos in bas-relief, followed by names of people who cared. The new Family Farm is selling memorial bricks and horseshoes for people to leave a record of their names, dates, and sentiments. It is a token of kindness, but real loving kindness nevertheless.

It's my belief that if I spend some time being nice, small measures of kindness waft through the air and bring goodness to the world. It can be a morning massage for my dog to ease that tight spot in her back, or a sprinkling of Parmesan on her kibbled dog food when she seems to need some cheering up. I can help a mother lift her stroller up the steep steps to the elephant overlook. I often let the children move up front to watch the crocodile come up to breathe even though I've been waiting for this for many minutes and wanted the good view. When I let someone else have the last chocolate cone and make do with the vanilla, it tastes that much sweeter.

Kindness reaps its own rewards. When you are kind, seratonin increases and your immune system gets stronger. The same is true when you are the receiver of kindness. And to top it off? The same is true when you simply *observe* an act of kindness. What would happen if with the price of admission, we brought into the entrance gates a deliberate act of kindness, a random act of kindness, or just a kind smile or a friendly look? What global force field would be set in motion in this park, in a piece of forest in a mid-sized northwest city?

I know that when our curators are in doubt, they choose to be kind. We saved an elephant seal that would never be able to migrate her usual 13,000 miles a year in the wild. Mira was born blind yet she greets people with a gentle-whiskered face and limpid eyes as she bobs up and down in Steller Cove. We know she'll be expensive to feed and time consuming to train and care for, but we tend to her with daily kindness.

We saved a bald eagle that would never have been able to hunt, fish and mate in the wild. Chinook has a damaged wing and cannot fly well, yet thousands of zoo visitors stand in awe as the Star Spangled Banner plays brightly and raises goose bumps on their arms. This magnificent creature coasts downhill on outspread wings, able to balance himself but not propel himself forward well, and is alive because we feed her, care for her, and choose to be kind.

Remember the romance novel? The heroine of the story moved to Hawaii and is now raising a child and loving a man because she chose to be kind. There's a keeper at the Oregon Zoo who has the patience of a saint and is a living example of how we can be loving and kind. There's a woman and an orangutan who healed each other by sharing a bond and taking the time to listen and be kind. There's you and I at the zoo on any one day, making choices that affect each other and our planet, because we make the choice to be kind. There are many questions in my own life about how to act, what to decide, or what road to take. The complexities of everyday life become very simple when I remember: "when in doubt, above all else, be kind."

Messages From the Deep

Love wells up as two dark shapes sink down in the snapshot I'm holding. It's a study in dark blues, turquoises and blacks. The sea lions serpentine diagonally across the photo, winding around each other in aquatic bliss. One has jet black eyes which look right at me. This creature draws me in and I cannot resist the pull. I slide the image back in the album and remember the day I took the picture. It was the day I fell in love.

Today I went back to grin like a fool, submerge myself in pleasure, and watch the objects of my affection. I sat on the carpeted step in front of the dimly lit underwater viewing area, writing pad in hand. I thumbed through my notebook of animal facts, read through training notes about animals in the cove, and gazed longingly at the rippling turquoise depths before me. Who was I fooling with my papers and books? They slid to the floor and I leaned forward, elbows on my knees and chin in my hands. I wanted to learn from these animals, not study about them. A muffled splash told me they had entered the water and in a moment, the two sea lions swung into view. They began their aquatic laps sailing towards me, veering off where the glass kept us apart and looping towards me once again.

There is much I know about these animals and this exhibit on the physical realm. I know it takes specialized gear and about 50 pounds of equipment for human divers to descend, clean the glass, and pick up foreign objects that have been pitched into the pool. I've seen the 60-pound boxes of "Instant Ocean" that provide salt and minerals to re-create the taste and tang of the sea. I've met the two technicians that work full-time to run the equipment and keep the water chilled and clean. I hear visitors rave about the beauty of the sapphire blue pools but the animals care more about the water chemistry which is checked on a strict schedule.

I've read the biographies of Gus and Julius, our Steller sea lions. They were born in California and Texas, and then moved to an aquarium in Connecticut. They were then flown by Federal Express with a veterinarian and keeper in attendance, to their new home in Oregon. Tipping the scales at about 1,000 pounds each, they're big likable fellows. Still, they're on the zoo's official "dangerous animal" list and a force to be reckoned with.

Gus and Julius are now residents of the Oregon Zoo and have settled in nicely. The in-house vets watch for scrapes and cuts, monitor their weight and nutritional needs, and keep a close eye on cataracts that are developing with advancing age. Sea lion dinner ingredients are shipped in by refrigerated trucks and quarantined in the off-site deep-freeze for at least 90-days to kill any harmful bacteria or parasites. Seafood is then transferred to the on-grounds commissary where boxes are filled each day to go to the keeper kitchen, a place rigorously scrubbed and sanitized according to USDA regulations. Herring, mackerel, capelin, squid and vitamins are the hand-fed rewards during training sessions, three times a day. The sea lions' operant conditioning program builds a vocabulary of behaviors that help man and beast work together. From this effort springs an exercise program to keep them fit, a target-training program for mental stimulation, and a routine that allows them to be participants in their own health care: annual exams, dental checks and routine blood work.

I know these facts, but I also take flights of fancy. My mind drifts as I become mesmerized in front of the three-inch thick glass. It's mighty enough to keep sea lions from hurtling through to my feet followed by 197,000 gallons of artificial seawater. Still, it's a frustrating barrier. I get up to press my nose to the glass so that it all but disappears.

Secretly, I want to get in there but only certified divers are allowed. It's one of the most coveted volunteer opportunities at the zoo. There's something thrilling about being underwater with the aid of SCUBA tanks, defying nature's rules that say we need air. We are weightless just like during our nine-month sojourn in the womb, and there is comfort as well as magic there. Sounds are muffled and all we hear is the rumbling exhale of bubbles coursing through our mouthpiece before erupting out into the water in a burst of silver champagne. Our bodies become graceful as we glide, and slight currents push and bend our spines so we can swim like supple, shimmering fish. What would it be like to be a graceful sea lion rather than an awkwardly paddling human encased in neoprene?

They say that each animal has a story to tell. Animal behaviorists record barks and bellows and try to make sense of them. I'm more drawn to the shamans and medicine men who woo the spirits of the animals to come out and play. Instead of decoding the voices, they enter into dialogue with the essence of the animal. If we spend time listening, watching and being receptive, specific animal totems might glide into our days and anchor us to something real. We can watch, wait and long for them. But it takes time. When they finally arrive, we need to commune with them, re-learning a language that we've forgotten. It is a maddening process, yet somehow delicious. As the old saying goes, any good relationship takes work.

It is whispered that the animal chooses us, not the other way around. It is we who need their guidance, not they who need to be chosen and lofted high as talismans of our own making. Animal totems bring protection and direction, solace and inspiration, to those who seek it. Many native peoples in North America believe this. Ancient cultures in far away lands have celebrated this connection for eons through art, dance, stories, and ritual. Do some cultures have more gods and spirit guides because they see wisdom everywhere? I roam the zoo, peering through glass and netting, over railings and through wires, to find some wisdom for myself.

I have always been a seeker, and irresistibly drawn to the watery animal world of oceans and seas. As a child, I incessantly drew penguins, whales, octopi, and seascapes with waving kelp. When I was older and heard my first New Age recording of violins, piano and the soundings of a whale, I wanted to weep. I chose a university based on its proximity to the sea, and even today I take nightly baths pouring in Epsom salts by the capful as if to bring salinity into my very pores. I am unmistakably drawn to the sea creatures. Is the sea lion my totem? If I stand patiently, nose to the glass in the dim light, will I receive messages from the deep?

The sea lions sweep by again and again in their underwater dance. At first, I see only dark shapes. Soon, I can make out the details. I see that Gus is a brownish gray. Julius is more red. They follow one another or swim in tandem. I can tell that Gus is younger, has keener vision, and is a tad more nimble than Julius. There is a protectiveness as they flow around the rocks, surface for air, and loop down again towards the glass. Gus leads, Julius follows. Whiskers and water currents feed back an endless stream of information about where one is in relation to the other. Gus is more apt to change his course and Julius is more often keeping to the staid and true. Gus pulls ahead and then hangs back impatiently, while Julius is steady, just gliding along with an internal rhythm that never wavers. All are intimate details, turning shapes into personalities, facts into something real that I can notice and relate to.

I am drawn to Gus because he is more like me – a leader, in charge, athletic and strong. I continue to watch, and bit-by-bit, words leave me. My head empties and my body becomes a clear vessel through which feelings and sensations can flow. I imagine what it would be like to have a powerful torpedo-shaped body like his. With an effortless sweep of my flippers, I would glide beside the rock pilings and brush my whiskers against the glass on my return trip around. I could drift my eyes shut and just feel the brush of cool waters against my skin, or open them and see through the haze of swirling waters and the opacity of reflective glass to the shapes and colors of humans just beyond. I could feel the vibration of footsteps and the higher-frequency thrum of voices. Perhaps I could even hear an indrawn breath or feel the heat of bodies as a new group of visitors come to gape in awe.

Something comes over me. A powerful energy soars through and I am catapulted through the water like a cannon ball. A momentary panic ripples through my long body because I am not accustomed to this pace. The fear falls away in a moment, though, and I feel pure power and delight. I sense Gus, rather than see him, and swing to his side. My whiskers touch his flank and we hurtle on, rounding a turn, diving down, and then shooting up for a breath of air. The sunlight shocks my eyes closed and we dive again in tandem. I open my eyes but can hardly see, the cataracts on my eyes dulling everything to a cloudy sepia brown. I feel calm and confident though, trusting and secure, as we spin infinity signs and geometric shapes around the pool. I am suspended in the present, the now, the moment. I feel patient and steadfast. My mind is freed from the worry that has plagued me in a dim past that I can hardly remember now. In the depths of my mind, a thought forms. It is Julius. Julius is the totem who has chosen me! He can balance me and teach me what I need to know: patience, teamwork, and the ability to trust life and lovers to walk with me when my vision is not too clear.

A baby carriage bumps my foot. An infant wails. I smell apple juice and Ritz crackers and I'm snatched back into present time. The mother begs my pardon. I nod and smile and I pick up my papers and stumble out into the light. It takes me a while to regroup, walk upright, and jostle shoulders with other human beings. Meeting animal totems is not for sissies!

Up the ramp, I head for the viewing area where I can see the sea lions on land. Julius heaves himself out of the water and ripples his sleek and majestic body up to the beach. It is his nature to spend part of his time in water and the other part on land. When water shows up in our dreams, it symbolizes creativity, our active imagination and lucid dreaming. But we also must have our feet on something firm to lead a balanced and effective life.

I think about the essays I'm writing. Like a splash of cold water on my face, I see it is not enough for me to dabble around with words and ideas when I'm at the keyboard. Eventually, I need to put them together into something recognizable, and then pull them out of the creative waters to the land where the practical matters of printers, marketing, and buyers await. Female sea lions rise out of the sea to give birth on land and I, too, need to bring the creative force out from within and set it in motion.

I see Julius's glistening head and his tiny ears. Unlike seals, sea lions have external ears that we can see. They are Julius's center for balance when he idles, suspended in the water. What is up, what is down, and which way does he want to go? I reflect on my own life and think of the dozens of choices I make every day in the name of balance: when to wake up, what schedule to keep, which people I will extend myself to, and what commitments I will make and keep. I live an enviable life with few responsibilities or restrictions. I keep up a creative tension by driving myself with passion, ambition and self-discipline to keep a tenuous balance between reflection and action. It is not a restful life, but a fulfilling one.

We live in a culture of freedom and opportunity. The malady that drives us almost to despair amidst all this abundance and prosperity is over-extending, over-spending, over-indulging. We get unfocused, chronically fatigued and misdirected. We can ask for guidance in keeping balance in our lives from these creatures that instinctively know where they are and where they're going. They travel far, migrating up to 13,000 miles each year in the wild. Surely, that unerring sense of where to go and the stamina to complete the journey is something they could talk to us about.

These small ears are also the way that Gus and Julius hear the clank of the gate hidden behind the rock walls that signal that the keepers are coming out with fish, the chatter of the ever-changing crowds, and the calls of the gulls which may have drifted 100 miles inland to circle around the zoo. My animal totem book says that sea lions in my dreams are sent to remind me to listen to my inner voice. I put serious effort into cultivating my intuitive sense although I love the certainty of financial spreadsheets, my day timer, and detailed timelines for writing projects.

My friends and I are playing a game where we're writing down a current challenge in our life and then asking for a "sign." We might have a dream, feel an inner urging, see a message on a billboard, overhear a conversation, or have a synchronistic series of events that lead us to an answer. Recently I've been noticing a lot of signs that say "stop," "yield" and "slow down" and by resting more and taking time off, I find my life flows much better and is ultimately more productive in satisfying ways. There are many ways to hear. I can strain my literal and metaphorical ears seeking guidance to help me on my way. I am not alone in my life journey if I listen to guidance from other realms.

A couple nearby is newly in love, silly, giggling and awkwardly holding hands. The zoo is a place for romance. Its signature seasons are spring and summer when hormones soar and lovers come out in droves to spend time on the wild side. I've had romance at the zoo myself — a brief and heady relationship last year where we visited the zoo at least a dozen times. Then there were a couple of Internet dates, both ending ignominiously at the parking lot — one man I had a fleeting interest in said "I'll call you," and never did. The other I had to write a painful "Dear John" e-mail to since he shared my curiosity about the zoo but not an iota of my passion.

Thank goodness that animal totems like romance, too. Is this not an area of our lives where we could all use a little guidance? They creep, climb, and swim into the lives of irrationally emotional humans, and many couples are ecstatic that they share an animal totem. It's a steady undercurrent of commonality, welcomed to a partnership that by its very definition will have differences to be dealt with. We enjoy the outer trappings of romance like roses and dinners, yet love is an inner journey that brings us together and finds resonance there.

Animals teach us to express what is in our essential nature. Gus leads; Julius follows. Gus is ambitious; Julius is wise and rides the proverbial tides. By rediscovering our authentic selves, we can present to one another what is real and true about ourselves and have a better chance at a good pairing. Many theologians say that love is a stronger force than fear. Much of our lives might be about exploring this complicated paradigm. We hunger for closeness yet are often terrified of true intimacy. We need the courage to merge and compromise, yet also to take full responsibility for our own lives — a balancing act of the highest order.

I lead zoo tours after dark in an overnight experience for children. I remember one of those magical nights. The grounds were quiet except for the gurgle of water spilling into a reflecting pool, the rustle of bamboo, and a far-away call of a night creature deep in the woods. We round the corner from the tide pool and begin to wind our way back to the classrooms to roll out our sleeping bags and call it a night. The kids are tired but excited, enjoying the nocturnal adventure.

Another staff member goes ahead and tiptoes back, telling me in an excited whisper that the sea lions are sleeping. The kids creep forward, too tired to punch and giggle but able to pull themselves together for one more amazing sight before they head back to camp. The first stars push their way through the velvet of a darkening cobalt blue sky. Soft lights glow from the exhibit. The water shines like a mirror. We sneak forward and see Gus and Julius, a stone's throw away, snoring deeply as they slumber on the water's surface. We lean over the railing to see their whiskers and hear the whoosh of their breath. If we look carefully we can see the pulse ripple their fur as their hearts beat deeply in their chests. Wow!

We tiptoe away and head for our camp, a warm classroom. It will be stuffed with 30 over-stimulated kids and eight exhausted parents. It will smell like popcorn and hot cocoa. My tired body will rest on a microscopically thin pad in a sleeping bag smelling of mothballs and closet dust. The sounds of children's giggles and sleepy whispers will lull me into a restless sleep. I have no children and no spouse, yet it feels like we are family here, enjoying a camping adventure that is a rite of passage into the exploration of what is wild and true. It is a departure from my everyday life, yet somehow more genuine – sleeping as a group, having been bathed by a glowing moon and winking stars, and hearing the social chattering of siamang monkeys and the call of a lone peacock as we drift off to dreamland together.

Back at the cove, Gus and Julius turn slow pinwheels in the water as they sleep, tips of flippers touching one another. Sea lions naturally migrate for long distances and are adept at sleeping in the open seas. In their pool they slumber, transported to the mighty Pacific Ocean in their dreams while imaginary fish sweep by in schools deep below and petrels wheel soundlessly overhead. The sea lions' flippers wag slowly to keep them upright, and their heads raise and lower to take sleepy draughts of air before sinking just below the surface. Something startles them and they awake, instinctively seeking out each other before they begin to swim.

Their sleek coats glisten like the chunk of obsidian I have by my front door — a massive stone of protection that I symbolically placed there to ward off the untoward before it enters my life. But when you swing open the gate of my white picket fence, you'll see an even larger slab of rose quartz glowing pink and silver in the moonlight. It is the stone of love, of mystical guidance, and of messages from the deep. Alone, we are but one-winged angels. It is only in the arms of another that we can truly spread our wings and fly. Gus and Julius glide in tandem, flippered arms encircling one another as they soar through the watery depths, around the rocks, towards the glass, and then rocket away into a dark sea made of Instant Ocean and dreams.

Order Form

For additional copies of this book, send $14.95 plus $3.55 shipping and handling to:

>Pavo Press
>822 NW Murray Blvd #107
>Portland, Oregon 97229-5868

Name: _____

Address: _____

_____

City: _____

State: _____ Zip: _____

e-mail: _____

Contact us for:
- Educational discounts
- The study guide for home-schoolers and educators
- The use of this book as a fundraiser

Feedback is welcome! Contact Becky Lovejoy, author, at la-beck@juno.com.